T0383940

Routledge Revivals

The Economic Position of the British Labourer

The Economic Position of the British Labourer

Henry Fawcett

Routledge
Taylor & Francis Group

First published in 1865 by Macmillan and Co., Limited

This edition first published in 2018 by Routledge
2 Park Square, Milton Park, Abingdon, Oxon, OX14 4RN
and by Routledge
52 Vanderbilt Avenue, New York, NY 10017, USA

Routledge is an imprint of the Taylor & Francis Group, an informa business

© 1865 by Taylor & Francis

Publisher's Note
The publisher has gone to great lengths to ensure the quality of this reprint but points out that some imperfections in the original copies may be apparent.

Disclaimer
The publisher has made every effort to trace copyright holders and welcomes correspondence from those they have been unable to contact.

A Library of Congress record exists under ISBN:

ISBN 13: 978-0-367-14228-5 (hbk)
ISBN 13: 978-0-429-03082-6 (ebk)

THE ECONOMIC POSITION

OF THE

BRITISH LABOURER.

THE ECONOMIC POSITION

OF THE

BRITISH LABOURER.

BY

HENRY FAWCETT, M.P.

FELLOW OF TRINITY HALL, AND PROFESSOR OF POLITICAL ECONOMY
IN THE UNIVERSITY OF CAMBRIDGE.

Cambridge and London:
MACMILLAN AND CO.
1865.

PREFACE.

THE following pages form a portion of a Course of Lectures, which I delivered in the University of Cambridge in the autum of 1864. For the convenience of the general reader, I have divided the various subjects discussed, into separate Chapters. It was necessary in addressing a class of students, to expound many of the elementary principles of Economic Science; I have thought that many of these expositions might be here admitted.

In the Chapter on Trades Unions and Strikes. an allusion is made to the trade outrages at Sheffield. I think it is only fair to state that I have

recently visited Sheffield, and after many inter-
views with both the Employers and the Employed,
I have come to the conclusion, that these outrages
have for some years been discontinued, and that
they are now most heartily discountenanced by the
working men.

TRINITY HALL, CAMBRIDGE,
October 1865.

CONTENTS.

THE ECONOMIC POSITION

OF

THE BRITISH LABOURER.

CHAPTER I.

Introductory Remarks.

I PURPOSE in the course of the following Lectures to describe the position of the British labourer. The subject, if I can do adequate justice to it, must be particularly interesting, and one which I consider to be peculiarly appropriate for discussion from a Chair of Political Economy. This science has often had to incur the reproach of being unpractical. The business man assuming a confidence which ignorance alone can give, contemptuously sneers at political economy, and assumes that he is in possession of a superior wisdom which enables him to grapple with all the practical affairs of life, unhampered by theories and unfettered by principles. Our science will therefore in some degree vindicate its claim to utility, if it can show that connected with the position of the British labourer there are rapidly arising questions which are destined to exert a powerful influence upon the production of wealth and upon the distribution of property in this country. Men of business are proverbially acute in observing causes from which result temporary fluctuations in the price of commodities, but they are the last to recognise the slow, but not less inevitable working of more permanent causes, which may perhaps be destined to remodel the social state of a country, or to revolutionise the conditions upon which commerce may be carried on.

One moment's reflection will suggest some of the economic problems which may arise for solution during the next few years. Ireland is becoming depopulated. The Irish have hitherto supplied much of the lowest kind of labour required in England. Our corn has to a great extent been reaped by them, but the day is probably not far distant when Ireland will require English labourers to reap her own harvest. Again, it may be observed, that as the commerce of England has developed, a line

of demarcation more definite and more difficult
to be passed has arisen between the employers
and the employed. This separation between capital and labour is unnatural, and must be pernicious. The hired labourer, as a general rule, has no
pecuniary interest in the success of the work in
which he is engaged; his faculties are not stimulated, his energies are not evoked. His life is
passed without hope, and a discontent must thus
be too frequently engendered, which, if not corrected, may jeopardise the stability of our constitution. If for an instant we consider the past,
we shall see how great are the changes which
have been wrought in our national industry. In
former times the English farmers generally cultivated their own freehold estates. They were the
old yeomen of England who played so proud a
part in the annals of our country, and the yeoman
and his labourers often lived together, and thus
became attached to each other by some of the ties
of family affection. But three distinct classes, between whom no relation now exists except a pecuniary one, are at the present time concerned in the
cultivation of the soil. The landowner obtains the
greatest rent he can from his tenant, and the tenant
obtains from his labourers the maximum of work
for the minimum of wages. The employers and
employed are parties to a keenly contested bar-

gain, and the labourer therefore naturally endeavours to obtain the maximum of wages for the
minimum of work. I do not make this contrast
between the past and the present in the vain hope
of recalling a state of society which is irrecoverably
gone, and which could not exist at the present
time ; I do not wish to praise the past at the expense of the present. I am an earnest believer in
progress, but I have endeavoured by comparison
to exhibit in a striking light some of the salient
features in our present national economy, in order
to show that many circumstances of vast importance in their ultimate consequences are beginning
to affect the position of the British labourer. For
instance, are our agricultural labourers likely to remain permanently contented with their present
lot ? Theirs is a life of incessant toil for wages
too scanty to give them even a sufficient supply
of the first necessaries of life. No hope cheers
their monotonous career: a life of constant labour
brings them no other prospect than that when
their strength is exhausted, they must crave as
suppliant mendicants a pittance from parish relief.
Will generation after generation be content to pass
the same dreary existence, when in other countries,
with a climate as healthy as our own, with institutions as free, they may at once become landed-
proprietors, and they may see definitely placed

before them a career of affluence and prosperity?
Are there not sufficient indications to make us
reflect that if things continue as they are, an
English exodus may be imminent? England has
safely weathered the storms of political revolu-
tions. Centuries have passed away since the
foreign invaders stepped on these shores, but our
greatness cannot be maintained, our wealth cannot be produced, if our labourers in large numbers
leave our shores; for it is their strong arms and
their acquired skill which have achieved the mar-
vels of our material greatness, and which have
won for England glorious victories in every quarter of the world.

Whenever our labourers emigrate, it may be
safely concluded that they are prompted to do
so in order to improve their material condition.
People have often been driven from their country
by the despotic acts of their rulers; but an Englishman does not expect to find in other countries a
government more free, and he loves his native
land so dearly that he cannot leave it without
enduring many a bitter pang. Political Economy
is therefore intimately concerned with any discus-
sions which relate to the condition of the labourer;
for the object which this science has in view, is to
investigate the laws which regulate the production
and distribution of wealth. On every side we are

met with the most conclusive evidence that the production of wealth in this country is so vast and so rapidly augmenting that it is idle to say poverty exists because enough wealth is not produced. I will not weary you with figures, I will only remind you that during the last twenty years our foreign trade has more than trebled; and if you wish for any further proof of the increase in our national wealth you can yourselves observe the vast manufactories and warehouses which have been erected, the mighty docks which have been opened, and the rapid extension throughout the country of railways, which bring wealth to every district through which they are carried. Everything therefore concerning the amount of wealth produced appears to be satisfactory, but a very different picture is exhibited if we reflect upon the way in which this vast wealth is distributed. This augmentation of national wealth has not arrested the Irish exodus. Many classes of labourers have still to work as long, and for as little remuneration as they received in past times, and one out of every twenty inhabitants of England is sunk so deep in pauperism that he has to be supported by parochial relief The advance in the material prosperity of Liverpool, of Glasgow, and other centres of commerce is unprecedented, yet in close contiguity to this growing wealth there

are still the same miserable homes of the poor,
the same pestilential courts and alleys, where
fevers and other diseases are bred which deci-
mate the infantile population with unerring certainty. Here then is a political economical question of surpassing interest and importance to solve,
and the solution of which will form the basis of
our investigations. How is it that this vast production of wealth does not lead to a happier
distribution? How is it that the rich seem to be
constantly growing richer, whilst the poverty of
the poor is not perceptibly diminished?

In attempting to work out this problem, I shall
endeavour carefully to abstain from indulging in
any vituperation against either employers or employed. The chief object which I shall have in
view will be to describe the different economic
systems which may regulate the production and
distribution of wealth, and according as any economic system may prevail, I shall attempt to
explain what arrangements may be adopted so
as to bring the greatest happiness to the community in general. Thus in our own country
three distinct classes usually share the proceeds
of agricultural industry, viz. landowners, farmers,
and labourers. I shall compare this agricultural
economy with that of other countries where the
land is cultivated by its owner. Again, with regard

to our commerce and trade, the capital is almost invariably supplied by the employer, and the employed consequently work for hired wages. When the produce which the land yields is distributed, between the landowners, farmers, and labourers, the amount which is allotted to each of these three classes is regulated by definite laws which no artificial arrangements can permanently control. When the capital and labour which any industry requires is supplied by distinct sets of individuals, the relative amount which the employer receives as profits, and which the employed receive as wages, is also determined by precise and well ascertained laws. We shall therefore be naturally led to consider the condition of the labourer under two distinct aspects. We must not only investigate the various circumstances which may affect his position if he continues simply to work for hire, but we must also attempt to trace some of the many consequences which will ensue if the labourer advances into a different social position, and supplies some of the capital which his industry requires. Hence some of the topics can be readily suggested which will fall within the scope of our inquiries. For instance, I shall describe to you the landed tenure which prevails in England with the view of showing what are its effects on the cultivation of the soil, and what

is the influence it exerts upon those who are engaged in agriculture. I shall give you a detailed
account of the Co-operative movement, and the
facts which I shall adduce will prove that a new
industrial era has been inaugurated. I shall endeavour carefully to explain the functions of capital, with the view of showing you the causes which
regulate the remuneration of labour. You will
then be able to perceive that employers and employed would both be benefited by the introduction
of some system of Co-partnership between capital
and labour. I shall illustrate the necessity of improving the relations between masters and men,
by considering the influence which is exerted by
Strikes and Trades Unions. Finally, I believe the
full importance of the subject we are discussing
will be understood when some of the considerations
connected with emigration are laid before you.
Many countries are now competing for British
labour; if therefore the condition of our industrial classes does not improve, that labour which
creates our wealth, and maintains our greatness,
will be attracted to other lands.

CHAPTER II.

The Land Tenure of England.

IT is an admitted fact that at the present time in England the average size of farms is increasing, and that a large proportion of the aggregate land in the country is gradually passing into the hands of large proprietors*. Before we trace the consequences of these changes, it will be well to enquire whether they are produced by artificial regulations, or whether they are due to natural causes. It will not be difficult to distinguish between the natural and artificial causes which exert an influence to accumulate the landed property in this country in the hands of a smaller number of proprietors. Those causes which are artificial are the laws which affect landed property, and these laws cannot be justly continued if it can be shown that they are not advantageous to the general

---

* It has been calculated that a century since, there were three times as many landed-proprietors in England as there are at the present time.

community. The theory of our constitution as it
now exists, is based upon the supposition that it is
desirable that one of the powers in the State should
be an hereditary aristocracy, and it is assumed
that an hereditary aristocracy cannot be maintained unless they are the owners of large landed
estates. Our law therefore confers on a landed
proprietor facilities for preventing the subdivision
of his estate, and everything is done to encourage
the feeling that it is desirable that landed property should not be subdivided. If a man dies
without a will his landed property passes intact
to his heir, whereas his personal property will pass
in part to his widow, and the remainder is divided
equally amongst his children. If he had no children, his property would be distributed in certain
fixed proportions amongst his relations. We must
therefore inquire what are the effects which these
laws of property produce upon the general interests of the nation.

I am desirous to make my remarks as little
political as possible, and I will therefore assume
that we unanimously admit the impolicy of making
any radical change in our constitution. We are
anxious that our Parliament should continue to
consist of two assemblies, one elected and the
other permanent. The history of the past has
repeatedly shown that if legislative power is en-

tirely confided to an elected assembly, there may
be no influence to withstand the outbursts of popular passion. We will therefore admit that nothing
ought to be done to jeopardize the existence or
to weaken the influence of the House of Lords,
so that there may be always a power in the State
to exercise calm and deliberate wisdom, if the
representatives of the people, reflecting the excite-
ment of their constituencies, should be hurried into
hasty and unjust legislation. But if we make
these admissions, does it follow that in order to
have an assembly which shall possess the functions
of the House of Lords, we must maintain laws
whose avowed effect is to keep intact the estates
of our landed aristocracy ? Every feeling in our
nature is opposed to the idea that one child in
a family should be selected for special favour, and
that he should be enriched, whilst his brothers
and sisters are made comparatively poor. If a
man had £100,000, and left £90,000 to his eldest
son, and divided only £10,000 amongst his four
remaining children, every one would denounce
such a disposition of property as most unjust and
most unfair ; but if a man had an estate worth
£100,000 and left the whole of it to his eldest
son, he will do exactly what our law would do for
him, if he died without a will ; for the law of
England interprets a man's natural desire to be,

that all his landed property should pass to his eldest son, even although his other children may be left entirely unprovided for.

Since the inheritance of landed property by one child to the exclusion of others, although encouraged and facilitated by our law; is manifestly opposed to all our conceptions of justice, it follows that primogeniture cannot be defended, unless it can be clearly proved to bring to the State some decidedly compensating advantages. Those who assume that the House of Lords cannot exist without primogeniture, may argue that our constitution cannot be preserved unless this institution is maintained. But I believe that the assumption implied in this argument is not correct. In order to secure the permanence of the House of Lords, nothing is so important as that there should be in this assembly some of the ablest men in the country. The intelligent people of England would quite as soon place faith in the divine right of kings, as they would be induced to believe that a man inherits by birth any claim to legislate for them. The existence of the House of Lords will never even be threatened as long as it can be shown that its functions are exercised wisely and efficiently. At the present time 428 peers have a right to sit in that assembly. And yet out of that number perhaps not more than

40 or 50 have either the taste, or the inclination, or the capacity to take the slightest part in its deliberations, even when the gravest political questions are discussed. If hostility should ever be shown towards the House of Lords, it will not be because the English nation desires the abolition of a permanent legislative assembly ; but no one need be surprised if the day should arrive when the nation will not tamely submit to see the fortunes of the state controlled by the votes of men who give their proxies to a party leader, because they are too careless or too indolent to be present, when questions of the gravest importance upon which they have to decide are discussed. The House of Lords would have been long since destroyed by those peers, who either from indolence or incapacity do not perform their hereditary legislative functions, had not that assembly been constantly renovated by illustrious commoners who have achieved distinction either in arms, literature, politics, or science. In a free and enlightened country no body of men will be permitted to exercise legislative power simply because they have inherited rank and wealth. The friends of an hereditary aristocracy advance a dangerous argument, if they assert that the existence of the House of Lords depends upon the maintenance of the large landed estates of our peers. Edu-

cated people will rebel against such opinions; it
will reasonably be said, that ability, education, and
leisure, may give a man a claim to be a senator;
but that any principle of inheriting political power,
unless it secures these qualities, cannot be advantageous to the State. The remarks which have
just been made may, I think, be considered to
lead to the two following conclusions: first, the
maintenance of the House of Lords does not depend on primogeniture; secondly, our laws of real
property which facilitate the inheritance of land
entirely by the heir, cannot be maintained upon
the plea that they tend to preserve the constitution
in its present form; for our House of Lords would
be more permanent and more efficient if such a
large proportion of its members were not placed
there simply because they inherited rank and
property.

I think therefore enough has been said to justify the conclusion that no political considerations
of paramount importance demand that our present
laws of real property should be maintained. As
we have now disposed of the political part of this
question, we have next to investigate the economic
consequences which result from permitting such a
disposition of land as now prevails in England.

I have already referred to the extraordinary
circumstance that if a man dies without a will,

our law interprets his desire to be, that his landed property should pass intact to his heir. In the case of intestacy, a broad line of demarcation is drawn between land and all other kinds of property; in fact, the law seems to be framed with the view of encouraging the opinion that a landed estate ought to pass undivided from generation to generation. You will observe how these sentiments have affected the whole law of this country, as we proceed to consider the control which a man who makes a will is permitted to exercise over the future disposition of his landed property. Thus a landowner can leave his estate to an unborn child. *A*, we will suppose, leaves an estate to his son *B*, on the condition that at *B*'s death the estate should pass to *B*'s eldest son. This is what is termed entailing an estate; and amongst our landed aristocracy it is almost invariably the custom to create successive entails. Thus, when *B*'s eldest son comes of age, the estate is again settled upon his eldest son, who may be a child unborn. Now it is at once evident that this power of entail prevents a great part of the landed property of the country ever being brought into the market. For instance, *B*, who inherits a landed estate from *A*, has only a life-interest in it, and until his eldest son comes of age he cannot dispose of his estate as a freehold; he can simply sell his life-interest in it.

Of course when the eldest son does obtain his majority, he has a direct interest in preventing the sale of an estate which is settled upon him. It therefore clearly follows, that entailing estates is an artificial arrangement which prevents a great part of the land of a country ever being brought into the market. Now it appears to me that the government has a clear right to interfere if landed proprietors do anything with their land which is opposed to the general welfare of a country. The primary condition of individual freedom is usually assumed to be, that a man should do as he likes with his own; but I conceive that if this meaning is given to ownership of land, no one can be fairly considered to be the owner of land. Parliament is repeatedly affirming, that a landed proprietor has not a right to do what he likes with the land in his possession. Landowners, for instance, are constantly protesting against a railway passing through their property, but by Parliament these protestations are disregarded, and the railway is permitted to be made, because public convenience requires it. Again, history shows that from the earliest times the possession of landed property was always considered to carry with it some obligations to the state. William the Conqueror seized a great part of the land of this country, and distributed it amongst those of his followers who had most dis-

tinguished themselves in the field of battle. But
William never entertained the idea of giving any
one a single acre of land unfettered by any conditions ; he seems to have thought that those to
whom he gave the land, held it in trust for the
general good of the State; upon the landowners
devolved the duty of defending the country, and
he therefore ordained that they should be at all
times prepared to supply properly equipped soldiers, the number of whom should be fixed according to the quantity of land they possessed.

It is evident that the whole feudal system,
which so powerfully affected the constitution of
society throughout the middle ages, was based on
the principle that the ownership of land carried
with it certain obligations to the State. When
the feudal system was destroyed these obligations
were forgotten, and the numerous personal relations which formerly attached the baron to the
crown, and the vassal to the lord, were entirely
replaced by a series of pecuniary bargains. The
land-tax represents the armed support which the
feudal lord was bound to give to the crown. No
personal services now exist between landlords,
tenants, and labourers. The tenants simply pay
the rent, and the labourers receive the wages. I
have made these remarks, in order to show that
property in land was never originally conferred

without certain obligations being enforced. It therefore seems to have been conceived that there was a fundamental distinction between property in land and all other kinds of property, and this distinction, though perhaps not avowed, is clearly recognised at the present time. Thus, reverting to a former example, the State does not hesitate to take land for railway purposes when the public convenience demands it, although the owner may have the strongest objection to this appropriation of his property; but it would be an interference with individual freedom, which would not be tolerated, if the State should in the least degree attempt to dictate what a man should do with his personal property. Furniture, money, and everything else which is defined as personal property, is owned in the sense that a man can do what he likes with it. I therefore conceive that property has been permitted to be acquired in land, upon the condition, either expressed or implied, that the government should have an undisputed right to interfere if land is devoted to any purpose which may prove detrimental to the general interests of the nation. It therefore follows, that any law which affects the distribution of landed property should be immediately altered, if it can be shown that it does not promote the welfare of the community. This at once leads us to inquire whether

we can establish any principle which will guide us
in determining the consequences which result from
the laws which, at the present time, regulate the
disposition of real property in England.

It seems to me to be a self-evident truth that
it is for the interest of the whole community that
the land should be cultivated with maximum efficiency, because it is indisputable that the more
efficiently land is cultivated the more abundant
will be food and all the other products of the soil.
National wealth will consequently be increased,
labour will be better remunerated, and the poverty
of the poor will be greatly diminished. We must
therefore ask ourselves whether or not primogeniture, so far as it is permitted and encouraged in
England, promotes the efficient cultivation of the
land. The avowed object of those of our laws which
maintain primogeniture is to prevent the subdivi
sion of large landed properties. I have already
explained that land when it is once entailed cannot for a considerable period be brought into the
market. A great part of the land of our country
is therefore in the position that it cannot be sold;
the consequences which result from these restrictions can easily be shown, by describing one or two
cases which have probably occurred within the
experience of us all. A nobleman, we will suppose,
and it is no imaginary example, is the tenant for

life of a large landed estate worth £20,000 per
annum. This estate is entailed, or in other words,
settled on his eldest son. The nobleman has many
other children. His position requires an expensive style of living, and he therefore spends nearly
the whole of his annual income. When he dies
his eldest son will be the heir to a great property,
whilst his brothers and sisters will be extremely
poor. We do not wish to dwell upon this in-
equality, which is contrary to all our feelings of
natural justice; we wish here rather to inquire
whether the estate owned by a person in the position we have just described is likely to be cultivated with maximum efficiency. The owner, though
possessing a large income, must be considered to
be a poor man, because, since all his property is
settled upon his heir, he is able to make no
adequate provision for his other children. A poor
landowner has not the requisite capital to carry
out improvements on his estate, and even if he has
the capital he has every inducement not to spend
it, because by doing so he enriches the eldest son,
who will be wealthy, at the expense of his younger
children, who will be comparatively poor. We can
readily understand how powerfully these motives
may operate ; for instance, the owner of an entailed
estate may have certain land which it will be most
profitable to irrigate. £20,000 expended in irriga-

tion may double the aggregate produce obtained, and may yield a profit of 15 per cent. on the outlay. Although the owner of such an estate may fully understand how profitable such an outlay would be, yet he may fairly say, I am not justified in spending the money, because, in order to improve the property of my eldest son, I diminish the amount which I shall have to leave to my younger children. The whole nation therefore suffers a loss, because land, which might be made fertile, is thus kept in a state of infertility.

There are numerous other ways in which the entailing of an estate may impede the production of wealth; thus, the owner of such an estate may know, that it would be extremely profitable to plant a certain portion of his land. For instance, there has been for some years a rapidly increasing demand for railway-sleepers; consequently many highland proprietors have found it much more re-munerative to convert pasture into larch forests; but if they do so, they are of course obliged to make a temporary sacrifice in order to realize a large ultimate gain. The owner of an entailed estate may therefore feel that he cannot in justice to his younger children make this temporary sacri-fice of income; for if he should die before his larch trees came to maturity, his eldest son would enjoy the whole profit which would result from the sinking of a certain amount of capital, which might have been distributed amongst his younger children. Numerous other examples can be readily suggested, all of which combine to prove that the entailing of estates frequently prevents the efficient cultivation of land.

Again, it can be easily demonstrated that it is most highly detrimental to the general welfare of the nation, that the land of our country should be so rarely cultivated by those who own it. Large landowners seldom trouble themselves with farming. They may perhaps have a model farm near their country mansion, but the great bulk of their land is let at a fixed rent to tenants. It is impossible that such an arrangement can promote good cultivation, because the farmer who rents land has not so great an inducement as he ought to have, either for the outlay of capital, or for the exercise of energy and skill. Tenant farmers may very reasonably say, We would most gladly spend more capital in improving our farms, if we had any security that at the expiration of our leases our rents would not be so much raised, that our landlords would be able to appropriate to themselves the whole of the improvement which has been effected on their land by the outlay of our own capital, or by the exercise of our energy and skill. This feeling has not unnaturally stimulated

the farmers of Ireland to demand a tenant-right.
They say the law ought to provide a security that
a tenant farmer should enjoy the full benefit of
the improvement which he may have conferred
upon land by the application of his capital and
skill.   This demand for a tenant-right has always
been refused by the English Parliament as a
most revolutionary proposal, but in one province
of Ireland, *viz.* Ulster, the landlords, either from
fear or from a sense of justice, have so universally
conceded this tenant-right, that it has now become
a custom which has almost assumed the authority
of a law.   The evil which this tenant-right attempts to cope with is no doubt a real one, and
may be regarded as denoting a very serious defect
in our national economy.   It is however an evil
which has to a great extent been created by the
power of entailing land, for the avowed object of
an entail is to prevent the subdivision of estates;
and as long as so great a portion of the area of
this country is aggregated into large properties,
land will continue to be cultivated as it is now,
almost invariably by those who do not own it.

From these considerations, I think it must be
concluded that the system of entail is economically very disadvantageous, because whether large
farming or small farming is adopted, the land will
be rarely tilled with maximum efficiency, if he

who cultivates the soil is not also its owner; moreover, it appears to me self-evident, that if entails were not permitted, a much greater amount of land would be brought into the market. If however it is admitted that land would be generally cultivated better by its owner than by a tenant, it might be further concluded, that a man who purchased land with the view of cultivating it, would be able to afford to pay a higher price for it, than a man who wished to purchase the land with the view of letting it. It will perhaps be rejoined, that although we have a law of entail at the present time, yet land is constantly brought into the market to be sold to the highest bidder, and that therefore nothing prevents those farmers purchasing land who possess the requisite means, and who also desire to become landed proprietors. But a farmer who buys land with the view of cultivating it will look upon the transaction simply as a commercial one, and will not therefore become a purchaser if the price of the land is artificially raised by any extraneous circumstances. Now the desire to possess land is inherent in man. Its ownership gratifies some of our most natural and admirable tastes. An opportunity is thus often given to study Nature in her most pleasing aspects, and the ownership of land enables all those pleasures of a country life to be enjoyed which are so thoroughly congenial to Englishmen. The possession of a large estate gives social position, and also often confers considerable political influence. The successful trader, or the lucky speculator, may try in vain to advance his social position even by the most lavish expenditure of wealth in London; but if he becomes a large landed proprietor, his position in society will be rapidly ensured; he is soon made a county magistrate; he will then rank as a country gentleman, and his sons may perhaps reasonably look forward to represent the county; and they will thus gradually enrol themselves amongst the landed aristocracy.

All these advantages which we have enumerated as belonging to the ownership of land, of course possess a pecuniary value, because people are willing to pay a price for whatever may give them enjoyment. The price which is paid for these collateral advantages which attach to the possession of land depends on demand and supply. If there are five such successful traders or lucky speculators as those we have described, all anxious to purchase a particular estate on account of those indirect advantages which it will confer upon them, the price of the estate must rise far above its agricultural value: it is therefore manifest that this rise in price must be greatly increased by the law of entail, because when entails are permitted, a much smaller number of estates are brought into the market. Again in England the price of land will each year rise more and more above its agricultural value, because the population and wealth of England are rapidly increasing. The pleasures of a country life were never so highly esteemed as they are now; railways give men facilities for combining town occupations with residence in the country; it therefore follows that each year there are a greater number of people desirous to possess land, and each year they are willing to pay a higher price for it; consequently the price of land in England has a constant tendency to rise above its agricultural value: its agricultural value being determined by three circumstances, the value of agricultural produce, the expense of cultivation, and the current rate of profit. Hence it appears that the price of land is being constantly forced beyond its agricultural value by powerful causes, some of which are natural, and some artificial. The artificial ones are those which can, and ought to be controlled. Those who desire to purchase land with the view of cultivating it, cannot afford to pay a price which greatly exceeds its agricultural value. An additional argument is thus suggested against our present system of landed tenure; for the amount of land annually brought into the market is much less than it would be if the power of entail was restricted, and if primogeniture was not encouraged by our laws of intestacy. But if the quantity of land annually sold is diminished, land becomes a commodity so scarce that it assumes the character of a monopoly, which the rich will purchase as a luxury; under these circumstances, it is evident that land can be rarely acquired by those who desire to obtain a livelihood from its cultivation.

In our previous remarks it has been tacitly assumed that the cultivator is a capitalist farmer who employs hired labourers; but in many countries a great part of the land is occupied by peasant-proprietors, who may be regarded as small farmers cultivating their own land. The peasant-proprietors were formerly a numerous class in England; they were the ancient freeholders who in bygone ages played a proud part in our history; they were loyal, but they loved freedom dearly; they were the constant defenders of our liberty, and in many a hard-fought battle they made the name of England honoured and respected. But the class has now become almost extinct. Its last representatives are some small proprietors in the lake-districts, who are termed states-men. I know many villages where a century since there were thirty or forty of these small freeholders, whereas now the whole land of the parish has been aggregated into one large property. Political economists and agriculturists of high authority express the most opposite opinions with regard to the effects which result from peasant-properties. English writers, who are opposed to a system of small farming, are often induced to speak disparagingly of small landed properties. It is however most important to remember that there is a fundamental distinction between the small farmer who rents his land and the small farmer who owns the land which he cultivates. In this distinction are involved all the advantages which various writers have attributed to peasant-properties.

I am quite ready to admit that when land is rented, large farming compared with small farming is every year, in this country at least, becoming more advantageous. Costly machinery is now used in agriculture with the most beneficial results. Almost the whole of our corn is now thrashed by steam, and the flail will soon be a forgotten relic. The steam-plough is being gradually brought to a state of perfection, and the greater part of our land will doubtless in a few years be cultivated entirely by steam. The steam-plough requires a considerable area to work upon; it is almost useless in small enclosures, and it is moreover a very expensive implement. It could therefore with

difficulty be applied if the country was split up
into small farms, and a small farmer would rarely
have sufficient means to purchase so costly a machine; and even if he borrowed one his appliances
would be inadequate to employ it profitably.
There are also numerous other disadvantages
which attach to small farming. A flock of sheep,
whether numbering 300 or 600, requires an expe-
rienced shepherd, and therefore the wages paid for
superintending a flock of 600 would be little more
than half the wages which would be paid if the
farm was divided into two and a flock of 300
was kept on each. Again, the work which a
farmer who employs labourers does himself may
be regarded as labour of superintendence, and a
farmer can probably superintend 600 acres as well
as he can superintend 300 acres. From these and
various other considerations we are led to the
conclusion that large farming is more economical
and more advantageous than small farming. But
in comparing these two different systems of agriculture, it has been assumed that the large as
well as the small farmer employs hired labourers;
and if this is so, I think that the efficiency of both
these systems of agriculture may seriously be
impeded by a circumstance which though rarely
dwelt upon yet seems to me to be one of radical
importance.

The agricultural labourers of this country usually work for fixed hired wages. The farmer supplies the capital, and he is entitled to all the
produce which the land yields after paying all
the expenses of cultivation, which include rent to
his landlord and wages to his labourers. The
fundamental defect in this arrangement arises from
the fact that the labourers, because they do not
participate in the profits which their industry yields,
have no interest in the work in which they are
engaged. The labourer has no pecuniary motive
to work with energy and skill; there can therefore be little mutual sympathy between the employer and the employed. They too frequently
regard each other as antagonists in a keenly contested bargain; for it is the interest of the employed to do as little work for the wages he
receives, and it is the interest of the employer
to get work done at the smallest cost. It is difficult to form any adequate conception of the evil
consequences which result from this antagonism
between employers and employed. Work is frequently badly done, labourers do not exert energy
and skill, and the production of wealth is thus
seriously interfered with. Employers perhaps only
half recognise the loss which is thus inflicted upon
them when they complain that their labourers are
listless, that they shirk their work, and that they

care nothing for their master's interest. These complaints are more frequently, and probably more justly, made by farmers than by any other class of employers. Agriculture offers peculiar facilities for the negligent and indolent workman to escape detection. The labour is too scattered to be constantly watched. Every room in a cotton mill has an overlooker, who can at once see whether all the operatives are working as they ought, but the labourers on a farm are simultaneously engaged in various operations, and it is impossible that all of these can be properly superintended by the farmer or his bailiff.

I have now described the two most prominent defects in our present agricultural economy; the first of these arises from the fact that land in this country is so seldom cultivated by its owner. I have endeavoured to show that the only practical remedy which can be applied is to remove all restrictions which limit the amount of land that is brought into the market. The second great defect in our agricultural economy I have attributed to the fact that the industry of agricultural labourers is inefficient, because they merely labour for hire, and enjoy no share of their master's profits. It is therefore quite clear that these two defects are completely remedied when agriculture is carried on by peasant-proprietors. A peasant proprietor may be regarded as a labourer who owns the land which he cultivates. But now this question is suggested, Do any counterbalancing disadvantages arise from the cultivation of the land by peasant proprietors? In proceeding to discuss this question, we seem to be almost bewildered by the opposite opinions which have been expressed by writers of high authority. Our leading English economist, Mr John Stuart Mill, has collected the most elaborate evidence on the subject, and the conclusion which he has arrived at, is extremely favourable to peasant proprietors. On the continent the most eminent political economists, as well as the most eminent writers on agriculture, have been as decided in their approbation of peasant properties as Mr Mill. An opposite opinion, no doubt, very generally prevails in England; but it should be remembered, that continental writers speak with the authority which personal observation gives; for in many European countries, such as France, Flanders, Italy, Switzerland, and in parts of Germany, a great portion of the land is cultivated by peasant proprietors, whereas these small properties cannot be now considered to form a part of the agricultural economy of England. I will endeavour to give a brief summary of the arguments which have been urged on each side of the question; and I think I shall at least be able to show, that it is most unde-

sirable that our Government should sanction any
law, which virtually operates as an obstacle to peasant properties.

The discussion of this subject seems to me to
involve a comparison of advantages and disadvantages. On the one hand, there are the advantages
which arise from land being cultivated by its owner
without the assistance of hired labour; on the other
side, there are the disadvantages which result from
farming on a small scale, because a peasant proprietor must necessarily be a small farmer. This
being the position of the argument, a decision can
only be arrived at by appealing to experience.
We will therefore see what light can be thrown on
the subject by the consideration of undisputed
facts. The well-known Arthur Young, who is perhaps the most eminent of our writers on agriculture,
was a most decided opponent of small farming.
Any opinion which he expresses in favour of small
farming is therefore entitled to peculiar consideration. In describing his travels through France he
makes the following observations: " Leaving Sauve,
I was much struck with a large tract of land seem-
ingly nothing but huge rocks, yet most of it enclosed and planted with the most industrious attention. Every man has an olive, a mulberry,
an almond, or a peach-tree, and vines scattered
amongst them, so that the whole ground is covered

with the oddest mixture of these plants and bulg-
ing rocks that can be conceived. The inhabitants
of this village deserve encouragement for their industry; and if I were a French minister they should
have it. They would soon turn all the deserts
around them into gardens. Such a knot of active
husbandmen, who turn their rocks into scenes of
fertility (*because, I suppose, their own*) would do the
same by the wastes, if animated by the same omnipotent principle." Again, "Walk to Rosendal
(near Dunkirk), where M. Le Brun has an improvement on the dunes, which he very obligingly showed
me. Between the town and that place is a great
number of neat little houses, built each with its
garden, and one or two fields enclosed, of most
wretched blowing dune-sand, naturally as white as
snow, but improved by industry. *The magic of
property* turns sand into gold."

There would be no difficulty in obtaining from
other countries an abundance of similar evidence
with regard to the "magic effect of property," and
I think that such testimony clearly proves that
peasant properties are favourable to the production of wealth. In every country in which they
exist on a large scale, it has been remarked by the
most competent observers that the land is well cultivated, and yields more net produce than under
any other system of landed tenure. Although

the facts which have been brought forward to support this opinion may challenge refutation, yet it will not be surprising if they do not bring conviction to the English reader; for he probably will plausibly urge, that a great part of the land of England would soon be occupied by peasant properties, if they were economically so advantageous as we have here represented them to be. If the cultivation of land by small proprietors was more remunerative, land when divided would realize a higher price, and consequently whenever a large estate was sold, it would be split up into a great number of small properties; yet in England it is observed that exactly the reverse of this takes place; landed estates are growing larger instead of smaller; for, as we have before said, a tendency seems constantly to be at work, which causes a great number of small freeholds to be merged into one large estate. Our previous remarks will however explain this seeming anomaly. The agricultural value of an estate is not the only circumstance which affects its price. A considerable portion of the value of an estate arises from the social distinction or political influence which it confers, and also from the opportunity which it affords to enjoy the pastimes and pleasures of a country life. Any cause which limits the amount of land brought into the market, *pro tanto*, raises its price above its agricultural value; and in a country like our own, the price of land constantly advances more and more above its agricultural value, because, as the accumulation of wealth increases, a larger number of people can afford a greater outlay, in order to enjoy the pleasures which are associated with the possession of land.

There is also another circumstance which exerts no inconsiderable influence, and which prevents land being divided into small properties. Our method of conveying land is most cumbrous and most expensive, and in order to obtain a secure title the same elaborate processes must be gone through, whether the land is considerable or inconsiderable in extent. If, therefore, an estate of 1000 acres was sold in lots of 20 acres each, the aggregate expense of conveying these 50 small properties would form a very appreciable portion of the whole value of the land. It is therefore evident that in England the subdivision of land is impeded by various causes, some of which are natural, and others artificial. Even if it were desirable, it would be impossible to control those causes which are natural, for the owner of a large estate ought certainly to be permitted to sell it as a whole, if he thinks that by doing so, he can obtain a higher price. But the public and our legislators ought seriously to consider, whether those artificial restric-

tions can be justly maintained, which prevent the
acquisition of landed property by the people. I
assume it has been proved by the facts here adduced, that small landed properties promote good
cultivation, and therefore conduce to the production of wealth; but I shall be able to urge a still
more powerful plea in favour of small landed properties, when I compare the social and material
condition of the peasant proprietors with our own
agricultural labourers.

Before I mention any special facts bearing upon
the social effects which result from peasant properties, it may be well to remark, that the condition of
a man who can enjoy the entire fruits of his own
labour is in every respect superior to the condition
of one who is simply a hired labourer, and who,
consequently, has no direct interest in the work
upon which he is employed. The faculties of the
latter are never fully stimulated, his hopes are not
excited by success, his energies are not called forth
to contend with the difficulties and disasters to
which every employment is liable; his life is, in
fact, one of dull routine. It may be said that he is
spared many anxieties with which the labourer
who is his own master has to contend. But it is
almost a truism to assert that these cares and
anxieties are the most valuable instruments of education, and that without them the human faculties

can never be adequately developed. These general
observations may be corroborated by actual experience, at least in the case of an agricultural community. All writers on peasant proprietors bear
the most decided testimony to their incessant and
intelligent industry. In Switzerland, France, Flanders, and the Rhine-land, we are told that the
small proprietors who cultivate their own land economise their time with the most scrupulous care;
they earnestly strive to turn every half-hour to the
utmost possible advantage; they work early and
late, and their labour exhibits a watchfulness, and
a fostering attention, which is never acquired by
hired labourers. Magical is the influence which the
feeling of property exerts, and truly indeed has it
been said by Arthur Young, that it is potent enough
to turn sand into gold, and convert a desert into a
garden. So great is the industry of peasant proprietors, that some writers have alleged that they
are too industrious; that they are in fact too much
engrossed in the business of life. But it is with
reference to the prudential virtues that they offer
the most striking contrast to our hired labourers.
The worst paid workmen in this country are so
thoroughly reckless, that they seldom show any
foresight for the future; and many consequently
who are impressed with this fact have maintained,
that higher wages effect no permanent improve-

ment in the condition of the poor. They do not
save their increased earnings, but spend their money
either in drink or luxurious living. That this should
be the case can be a matter of no surprise whatever. There is no effect of ignorance more certain
than an almost entire absence of foresight; and the
life of a hired labourer can exert no influence whatever towards cultivating any of the habits of prudence. His poverty is so great, that he naturally
indulges in somewhat better living when he has
the means; and even if he should, by dint of
great sacrifice and exertion accumulate a trifling
amount of money, he very seldom has any eligible
opportunity of investing these savings. No definite prospect is held out to him that his savings
will ever enable him to occupy a different social
position. If a hired labourer saves twenty pounds,
he has no chance of investing it as capital in some
profitable employment; the only purpose to which
he can devote it is to place it in the savings-bank,
where he obtains something below the current rate
of interest. How much more powerfully would prudence be stimulated, if a definite prospect were held
out, that a labourer might in the course of time, by
means of his saving, secure a small landed property! The value of such an acquisition to the
labourer is not to be estimated by the amount of
wealth with which it enriches him. It makes him,

in fact, a different man; it raises him from the position of a labourer, and calls forth all those active
qualities of mind, which are sure to be exerted
when a man has the consciousness that he is working on his own account.

These remarks are corroborated by the unanimous testimony of the most competent authorities;
for it has been repeatedly affirmed that peasant
proprietors are invariably a most thrifty class, and
so anxious are they to accumulate capital that the
style of their living has often been erroneously
supposed to denote poverty, when it is simply the
result of great economy. The advantage to be
derived from saving is brought most distinctly
home to them. A small proprietor knows that if
he can save a few pounds, he shall be able to have
another horse or cow, or perhaps some new implement, and he is able clearly to foresee the profit
which he shall derive from such a purchase. Let
a man once feel how efficient the wealth which
he saves may become in producing more wealth,
and he is sure in future to exert himself actively
to accumulate capital. Mr Browne, who was a
few years since the English Consul at Copen-
hagen, has made some most interesting observations, with reference to the peasant proprietors of
Denmark. He bears the most decided testimony
to their thrift, and also to the superior comfort

in which they live. Thus he says, "The first thing a Dane does with his savings is to purchase a clock, then a horse and cow, which he hires out, and which pay a good interest. Then his ambition is to become a petty proprietor, and this class of persons is better off than any in Denmark. Indeed, I know of no people in any country who have more easily within their reach all that is really necessary for life than this class, which is very large in comparison with that of labourers."

A system of small landed properties has sometimes been condemned, because it has been supposed to encourage a reckless increase of population. Upon this point the late Mr Richard Jones was most strong in his denunciation; but although this political economist collected many most valuable facts, yet he was prone to make unsupported statements, and without assigning sufficient evidence, often called upon his readers to reject a theory, or to assent to some particular opinion. Mr Jones says, that the peasant proprietors are "exactly in the condition, in which the animal disposition to increase their numbers is checked by the fewest of those balancing motives and desires, which regulate the increase of superior ranks, or more civilized people:" But he gives no reason for this opinion, nor does he attempt to support

it by specific facts. Many other writers, besides
Mr Jones, have maintained that small landed proprietors must become gradually impoverished, in
consequence of the continued division of the land
amongst the children of each generation. It is
not unfrequently assumed, that a man will marry
directly he acquires a small landed property, a
large family will have to be maintained, and that
the father will be able at his death to make
little or no provision for his numerous children,
unless he either divides the land which he owns
amongst them, or else leaves the land to one of
his children, heavily encumbered with annuities,
to be paid to the rest. In order to disprove such
suppositions, we will in the first place, show that
all *à priori* reasoning would lead us to conclude
that the acquisition of property will act more
powerfully than any other circumstance to make
a class prudent with regard to marriage; we shall
in the second place adduce specific facts, bearing
upon the slow rate of the increase of population
amongst peasant proprietors.

The most casual observer may have remarked
that the poorest classes in this country show the
greatest imprudence in regard to marriage. As
a general rule, a man does not marry in the
middle and upper classes, unless he believes that
he shall at any rate be able to give his children

as good an education as he has himself received, and be also able to place them in a social position, similar to that which he himself occupies. The majority of men are accustomed to some particular style of living; and they generally refrain from marriage, if the increased expenses of married life would compel them to live in a manner which would not give them what has been aptly termed "their habitual standard of comfort." But the very poor are not influenced by any such considerations; they are not restrained from marriage by a desire to preserve a certain standard of comfort. What standard of comfort could the miserable cottiers of Ireland have had? Those who are accustomed to poverty, do not attempt to exercise any restraint with regard to marriage; and amongst such persons, population is only restrained by the great mortality which prevails amongst the very poor, and more especially amongst their children. But when a labourer becomes a landed proprietor, he is at once influenced by the same motives which render the middle and upper classes prudent with regard to marriage. A person in the middle class appreciates the value of the position he occupies; and he will not marry, if marriage will so impoverish him as to render it necessary for him to resign his social position. A small landed proprietor must be quite as forcibly convinced of the superiority of his own position, compared with that of a hired labourer; and he will be equally careful not to marry, if he considers that the expenses of a family would force him to give up this position, and would compel him to sell his land, and return to the ranks of the ordinary labourer.

We have moreover abundant evidence to prove that peasant proprietors are acted upon by these motives. Sismondi, perhaps more than any other writer, has been impressed with the evils which result to the poor from over-population, consequent on imprudent marriages; and his strong advocacy of peasant proprietorships is principally based upon the conviction, that the system acts powerfully to restrain population. His testimony with regard to France is extremely important, because in France the system of small properties is put to the most severe test, by the operation of the law, which enforces the equal division of landed property. Sismondi says, "There is no danger lest the proprietor should bring up his children to make beggars of them. He knows exactly what inheritance he has to leave them; he knows that the law will divide it equally amongst them; he sees the limit beyond which this division would make them descend from the rank which he has himself filled; and a just family pride, common to the peasant and to the nobleman, makes him abstain from summoning into life children for whom he cannot properly provide."

In contrast with these results, the effects of our own system of landed tenure may be correctly characterized in the following manner. The land is owned by comparatively few great landlords; it is occupied by tenants who have sufficient capital to cultivate large farms, and the labour is supplied by hired labourers, whose wretchedness is proverbial, and between whom and their employers there is none of that personal sympathy which can alone be secured by the feelings of common pecuniary interest. I know our agricultural labourers well, I have long lived amongst them, and I can therefore describe their condition with confidence. In those localities which are not contiguous to the manufacturing districts, the wages of an agricultural labourer during the winter months do not exceed ten shillings a week; he works hard, he is often exposed to inclement weather, and with these wages he cannot procure for himself and his children a sufficiency of the necessaries of life. He rarely if ever tastes meat more than once a week. I have known many able-bodied men, who have to go through a long day's fatigue, have nothing for dinner, day after day, except tea and bread and butter; their strength is prematurely exhausted, and they often become old men at an age, when if they were better fed, they would be in the prime of life. Their condition always verges on pauperism. From such scanty wages, it is impossible to make any provision for old age or sickness. An agricultural labourer can rarely be found who has saved even a few pounds; he has to work with the regularity of a machine. No hope of more prosperous days cheers his monotonous career; a miserable prospect stands before him; for he knows that when his strength is exhausted, he must come to the parish as a suppliant mendicant for relief. The cottages of these labourers are frequently so bad, that they scarcely deserve the name of human dwellings; all the children of the family are commonly huddled together in one bedroom; every decency of life must be ignored and forgotten; and against the vices thus engendered, an antidote is supposed to be provided by the Church, the school, and the patronising speeches which may be delivered by the resident proprietor at an agricultural dinner. I have no hesitation in saying that if labourers became in the same way as horses, the property of their employers, it would be advantageous in a pecuniary sense, to feed and house them better. It is no consolation that the

labourers of other nations endure as much poverty
as our own labourers; it must be remembered
that in England wealth is accumulated far more
rapidly than in any other country, and the misery
of our poor becomes more deplorable to contemplate when it is contrasted with our vaunted progress in civilization, and in material prosperity.

I think, therefore, that it is the imperative duty
of our legislature, to abolish all those artificial restrictions which impede the division of land into
small properties; for the observations which have
been made in these pages, though by no means
exhausting the subject, have established two pro-
positions :—

First, when land is cultivated by small proprietors, it is at least as well cultivated, and as productive of wealth, as when a system of landed
tenure like our own prevails.

Secondly, the condition of the peasant proprietor is in every respect superior to that of our
own agricultural labourers, both in its social, material, and moral aspects.

Many may very naturally suppose, that unless
the land is compulsorily subdivided, small proprietors, cultivating their own land, can never again
exist as a numerous class in England. But whether
this may be so or not, justice and policy would
still equally demand that all artificial restrictions

which limit the amount of land that is sold, should be abolished, so that every one may have the greatest possible facility of acquiring land. The first care of Government, and its ultimate end, should be to promote the happiness of the people, and it cannot be denied that the nation at large would be more happy, if the soil which has been given to it by nature was enjoyed by many, instead of being possessed by few.

I should be the last to advocate the compulsory division of land; I would not confiscate one single right of property; but I regard the aggregation of land in the hands of a diminishing number of proprietors, as a national misfortune; and I therefore think that our laws should no longer be permitted to encourage this growing evil. No one can deny that primogeniture is facilitated by the existing power of entail, and that it is also promoted by the high sanction which is given to it, by a law of intestacy, which affirms as a principle, that if a man dies without a will, natural justice demands, that all his landed property should devolve to his heir. So wicked and mischievous a principle ought no longer to be enunciated by the law of England: I do not desire that a man should be prevented leaving his property to one child if it is his wish to do so; but if he leaves no will behind him, then I maintain that our law

ought not to make the slightest distinction between real and personal property.   It may be
urged that such an alteration in the laws of intestacy, as is here proposed, would produce very little
effect; probably it will be said that men frequently
now abstain from making a will, because if they die
intestate, their property will be distributed in exact
accordance with their desires.   It will be therefore
argued that if the existing laws of intestacy were
changed, the great majority would at once make a
will; and that therefore this change in the law
would produce little effect, because intestacy would
become extremely rare.   But this argument, even
if its truth is admitted, provides no valid reason
in favour of the maintenance of those distinctions,
which our law upholds, between real and personal
property.   Men's actions are controlled by custom,
and social morality is often tested by conventionality.   A man cannot instinctively feel that he
ought to leave all his real property to his eldest
son, and thus enrich one child and impoverish all
the rest; custom and conventionality can alone
justify such a course of conduct; and is not the
custom perpetuated, and does not primogeniture
receive the sanction of conventional morality, when
the State, having to give effect to what ought to
be regarded as a man's right intentions and natural
desires, declares as a principle, that personal pro-

perty ought to be equally distributed, but that landed property should pass intact to the heir?

A change in the law of intestacy, ought to be the first department of the land question, which should be discussed in the House of Commons. Such a question could be brought forward with peculiar advantages. Its settlement would destroy a bad and mischievous principle, and would in its place establish a right and beneficial one. Moreover, it may be regarded as peculiarly fortunate that this important result could be achieved without in the least degree interfering with any right of property; for no one can think that he is harshly dealt with, if the fullest freedom is given to him, to devise his property as he likes. When this question has been settled, there will arise another, perhaps more complicated and difficult; for sooner or later, Parliament must consider whether or not the interest of the country demands, that the existing power of entail should be in any way limited. I have already explained that entails are at the present time created by settling estates upon unborn children. Consequently it can be readily shown that the only real effectual limitation upon entails would be to decree that no estate should be vested in an unborn child.

It is not necessary for me to repeat that by the operations of the system of entails, a considerable portion of the land of this country may be regarded as a commodity which cannot be sold. There are however other disadvantages connected with entails to which I will briefly allude. I have already remarked that the great cost involved in the transfer of real property in this country acts as a severe impediment upon the acquisition of small landed estates. Every one who has ever drawn a conveyancing deed, will be prepared to admit that although a registration of titles would prove extremely beneficial, yet the conveyance of land must always be complicated and expensive whilst such a vast number of interests are allowed to be created in a landed estate. Without entering into a technical legal discussion, it must be evident that the creation of these multifarious interests is greatly facilitated by permitting land to be left to a number of persons who are as yet unborn. Hence two objects would be effected by the limitation upon the settlement of landed property which we have here proposed. In the first place a greater quantity of land would be brought into the market; secondly, the acquisition of land in small plots would be rendered more easy, because the cost of conveyancing would be diminished. Moreover, the other legislative measure which we have advocated would tend to produce similar results; for if the laws of intestacy

were altered, the number of landed proprietors in
this country would inevitably be increased, because
primogeniture would operate with continually les-
sening effect if it ceased to obtain encouragement
by receiving a high sanction from the law of this
country.

Before proceeding to consider whether the legislative changes which have been here suggested
would be accompanied with counterbalancing disadvantages, I would briefly summarise some of the
remarks which have been made upon the results
which arise from the aggregation of land in great
and increasing estates. In the first place I endeavoured to convince you that these large estates naturally lead to a bad and mischievous
system of agricultural economy. A great portion
of the land of this country is settled either upon
unborn children or upon minors; those who are
in possession of the land have consequently often
only a modified interest in it. They are therefore
discouraged from investing capital in agricultural
improvements, and they have no power to sell the
land to others who might have the inclination and
the means to improve it. Again, estates are so
large, that the land can rarely be cultivated by
those who own it, and I have sought to prove to
you that this separation of the cultivation from
the ownership of the soil must be inevitably an

obstacle to good agriculture. But I have with particular emphasis described to you the condition of
those who are engaged as labourers in the agriculture of England, because I regard this as the most
important part of the whole subject. If capitalist
farmers find it each year more difficult to become
the owners of land, how remote must be the chance
that the labourer can ever obtain the possession of
a plot of ground. I have adduced facts which I
believe prove that the peasant proprietors of the
continent enjoy a prosperity which our own agricultural labourers can now never hope to attain.
There are however other manifold evils which result from our present agricultural economy. You
have no doubt often heard lamentations about the
improvidence of our labourers. If they are more
reckless than other classes of the community, depend upon it this is due to some cause which must
be attacked, if we desire to remedy the evil. The
cause can be easily discovered; for can we suppose
that self-denial and prudence will be practised by
those who feel that they cannot descend to much
greater poverty, and who also cannot see definitely
placed before them any real hope of raising their
condition? How rapidly would the character of
this portion of our population be changed if a man
could say, A few years of steady industry, accompanied with prudence, will enable me to save suf-

ficient to purchase a plot of ground, and thus own
the soil which I cultivate!

I cannot better illustrate the powerful effect
which such sentiments produce upon men's character than by relating to you a most suggestive
anecdote. A friend of mine, a very intelligent traveller, met, whilst in Italy, the agent of one of our
largest railway contractors. This agent had 12,000
labourers at work upon his various contracts. My
friend asked him whether he preferred as labourers,
Englishmen or Italians. His reply was as follows:
"I have no hesitation in saying, that I like employing Italians better than Englishmen; the latter
have, no doubt, greater strength and energy, and
have the power of getting through more work in a
day, but they often cause me much trouble and
loss, on account of their intemperate and imprudent
habits; on the other hand, I have always found the
Italians, from whatever part of the country they
come, are sober, thrifty, and industrious; they seem
invariably influenced by the strongest desire to
save sufficient to enable them to purchase a plot of
ground, and this makes them exceedingly frugal
and industrious. I am quite convinced that the
prospect of securing the possession of a small plot
of land exerts a most powerful and beneficial influence on their character."

Experience has in fact always shown that there

is no taste more firmly implanted in man's nature than the desire to become the owner of land. This being the case, I venture to put this serious question to those who uphold the present restrictions which impede the acquisition of land in this country:—I will ask them whether they have considered to what an extent our national greatness and happiness may be imperilled if the élite of our labouring population should be attracted to the United States, and to our Colonies. In those regions land is cheap, labour is highly remunerated, and the desire to become a landed proprietor is one which can be easily gratified.

I trust you will not think that I desire to forbid primogeniture; if a man wishes to leave all his real property to his heir, I would give him the fullest power to do so; but it will perhaps be said, that the maintenance of our constitution requires that primogeniture should be encouraged. I have already anticipated this argument, and I again assert that, in these days, the possession of land does not give the House of Lords its power. The chief enemies to the House of Lords are some of the Peers themselves; the stability and permanence of this venerable assembly is ever liable to be undermined by those who show to the country that they are too careless, too ignorant, or too much absorbed in pleasure, ever to exercise the legislative func-

tions to which they are born, except by placing a
proxy in the pocket of their party-leader. Those,
on the other hand, who cause the House of Lords
to be honoured and revered by the nation are
those who have proved their power and capacity
either in the camp, in the forum, or in the arena of
politics. A Lyndhurst, an Ellenborough, a Dalhousie, or a Canning, might check the hasty legislation of an elective assembly reflecting the excite-
ment of the people; but who will pretend to say,
that the influence which such Peers as these could
wield is one jot strengthened by the possession
of landed property? The House of Lords would
soon fall into a state of pitiable feebleness, if that
assembly was not constantly renovated and invigo-
rated by men who have won peerages by illustrious
services. If there be any one who wishes to see
that venerable institution swept away, he would
soon have his desire accomplished, if primogeniture
was allowed full scope, and none were admitted to
that assembly but those who had inherited the
right to be there. The people will never again
consent to think that the Peers have a right to exercise legislative power and to claim obedience,
simply because they are a landed aristocracy. The
House of Lords will be honoured and obeyed, as long
as it proves to the people that it possesses delibe-
rative wisdom, and calm and temperate judgment.

I have dwelt as little as possible upon the political aspects of the question, and I will now proceed to consider some economic tendencies, which may be regarded as likely in this country to prevent the increase of small landed properties. Although I have spoken very favourably of peasant properties, yet I have endeavoured impartially to compare the relative advantages of large and small farms. In many departments of agriculture, large farms when compared with small ones are likely to become gradually more remunerative as machinery is more extensively applied to the cultivation of the soil. In some cases however small farming will always continue to be productive, for experience has proved that if an industrial occupation requires constant care, delicate skill, and minute attention to details, these qualities are most efficiently supplied by the individual who is prompted by self-interest to be watchful and energetic. As an example, the vine and the olive cannot be successfully cultivated, unless their growth receives a tender and fostering care; hence those vineyards and olive-gardens succeed the best, which are not too large to be superintended by the watchful eye of the proprietor. Again in our own country, dairy-farming demands the utmost attention to minute details, and consequently a dairy is not likely to be very profit-

ably conducted if it is too large to be properly
looked after by its owner. It therefore appears
that the advantages which arise from producing
on a large scale, are not equally marked in all
departments of agriculture; it has however been
shown by the experience derived from continental
countries, that the disadvantages of farming on
a small scale, are more than compensated by the
many and varied beneficial consequences, which
result from the association of ownership with the
cultivation of the soil.

But even if it is admitted that large farming is
more profitable than small farming, it is still of
the utmost importance that land should, as far as
possible, be made a marketable commodity. The
most significant circumstance connected with the
industry of this country during the last few years
has been the establishment and growing development of cooperative institutions. No one who
has watched this extraordinary movement can
doubt that as our labourers advance in intelligence
and moral worth, a greater portion of our industry
will be carried on by that union between capital
and labour which is implied in the word Cooperation. The subject is so important that I shall
proceed in a future lecture to discuss it with great
care. After I have described to you the remarkable success which has been obtained by many

of these cooperative societies, and after I have
shown to you the conditions which mainly tend to
secure the permanent prosperity of these industrial
combinations, I am sure that you will agree with
me in thinking that agriculture is perhaps more
likely successfully to be carried on by associations
of labourers than any other industry. When you
become acquainted with some of the results which
have been already effected by these industrial
combinations, you will see that the day is not far
distant, when labourers who have the means and
the inclination to acquire land will be able to
surmount the disadvantages of small farming, by
uniting themselves into an association, in order to
purchase a tract of land sufficiently extensive to
be most profitably cultivated. We, who venture to express such opinions, shall no doubt be
encountered with the old objection, that we are
conjuring up visionary and impracticable schemes;
but we have facts on our side, for I shall show you
that in many departments of industry, where difficulties were met with, which would not have to be
encountered in agriculture, associations of labourers
have become the founders and conductors of establishments which are rapidly extending in importance and prosperity. These considerations will
greatly strengthen the demand which the people
of this country can urge in favour of abolishing

all restrictions which impede the acquisition of
land. As labourers gradually advance they will
feel that they have the power and the capacity
to raise themselves into an entirely different social
condition by forming cooperative combinations;
in this way, they will supply the capital which
their labour requires; they will thus become their
own masters, and enjoy all the profits, which
their industry yields. Our rural labourers will
rapidly show an anxiety to join the movement by
applying the cooperative principle to agriculture;
and if in agriculture the movement is checked
by artificial restrictions which would tend to
prevent these associations of labourers acquiring
the necessary area of land, then we may depend
upon it that these men will not stay here to enrich us by their industry, and to augment our
national greatness by their growing wealth and
prosperity; they will seek a home in far distant
regions where land is abundant, and where they
will prove that, if an Englishman has fair scope
for his energy and skill, he will soon raise himself from the poverty by which he may have
been depressed; and he will show, that he has
that in him, to entitle him to take the foremost
place amongst mankind.

Before closing these remarks upon the land-
question, I think I ought to direct your atten-

tion to one or two topics which are intimately
connected with the subject we have been discussing. You will remember that I have com-
mented upon the diminution in the number of
landed proprietors in this country; the record
however of this diminution will entirely fail to
give an adequate idea of the extent to which our
people have been divorced from the soil; not only
were our freeholders in past ages a numerous and
important class, but in those days the inhabitants
of almost every village, even if they did not own
land, possessed certain proprietary rights which
were valuable in themselves and from which resulted many social advantages. Formerly there
was scarcely a parish in England, which had not
its common. This was, as its name implies, a
tract of land, which was the joint property of all
the inhabitants of the village. Here they could
graze a cow or feed poultry, and here too was a
recreation-ground, so delightful that the pleasures
of the 'village green' have been immortalized by
some of our greatest poets. Unfortunately in the
year 1836 an Act of Parliament was passed with
the view of facilitating the enclosure of commons.
I believe that the legislature never passed a law
which will ultimately do more irremediable mischief.
The commons are being rapidly swept away.
Cottagers have now no means of keeping a cow,

a pig, or poultry ; the village games are gone; every acre of ground is carefully fenced, the beaten path of the frequented high-way cannot be left without committing the crime and incurring the penalties of trespass, and I have been too often pained to find that the turnpike road is now the only recreation-ground for village children. But perhaps it will be said that Political Economy ought to favour these enclosures because in this way land, which was comparatively waste, has been properly cultivated and thus the wealth of the country has been increased. But I doubt the fact that these enclosures have augmented the national wealth, and even if it could be proved that they have done so, Political Economy would not supply a single argument in their justification, if it could be shown that this augmented wealth has tended, not to promote, but to diminish the comfort and happiness of the people. For various reasons I am inclined to doubt that the enclosure of com- mons has caused a greater production of material wealth. In the first place I would observe that pasture land is every year becoming more valuable than arable land; the price of stock and dairy- produce must continue rapidly to advance with the growth of population, whereas the price of corn may be kept low by foreign importations. Many of these commons were rich pastures, and

the country may now be said peculiarly to want
the produce which they used to yield. Thus from
the commons at Cottenham was made the cheese
which has obtained such celebrity. These rich
pastures have been enclosed and many of them
cultivated ; the additional corn which may be
grown there does not compensate the nation for
the loss of this dairy produce; wheat can be imported, but our own country must supply us with
the dairy produce which we may require. But if
augmented wealth has not resulted from these enclosures, nothing remains to be attributed to them
but unmixed evil. Those who owned these common ' rights,' received in the first instance some
compensation which was generally most inadequate. The compensation which was thus received
could be, and was generally spent, and thus the
next generation obtained not the slightest remuneration for the loss. But as long as the commons remained those who had rights in them
possessed a property which could not be alienated.
Moreover the labourer who could keep a cow or
some poultry enjoyed luxuries which daily wages
will never place within his reach. A great injury
has thus been inflicted upon the poor, because
every one who knows the working classes will tell
you how much their children suffer, when they are
unable to obtain milk to give additional nourish-

ment to their scanty food. Important however as
these considerations may be, yet in some cases, evils
of incomparably greater significance have resulted
from the enclosure of commons. I will explain
my meaning by taking one striking example.

You are doubtless aware that Epping Forest
was a large tract of woodland country so near
to the metropolis, that in bygone days Royalty
here found a convenient place to enjoy the pastimes of the field. Those who lived in the neighbourhood had the right of pasturage. The Crown
however retained the right to keep and hunt deer,
and hence not a single acre of the forest could
be enclosed without the permission of the Crown.
The deer have of course long since vanished
before the advancing tide of population. The
proprietary rights of the Crown remained, and
consequently the people represented by the Crown
have for years considered that it was their undisputed privilege to walk through the pleasant
glades, and to wander about undisturbed amongst
the beautiful scenery of Epping Forest. But unfortunately, either through jobbing or blundering,
government officials have permitted a very considerable portion of the forest to be appropriated
by private individuals. Seldom is government
carelessness likely to prove more mischievous ; for
who can estimate the extent to which the toiling

myriads of the metropolis will be socially and
morally injured by the loss of such a delightful
recreation-ground? How can the health of dense
masses of population be maintained, if they can
never feel and breathe the air of Heaven unim-
pregnated by noxious vapours? How can a people continue to be contented and happy, if they
can never reinvigorate their exhausted energies by
some of the pleasures and amusements which the
country can alone afford? And finally let me ask,
How can human conceptions be elevated, how can
human tastes be raised above mere sordid and
worldly pleasures, when there is no opportunity
of feeling that inspiration which is derived from
the contemplation of the beauties and glories of
Nature? Fortunately all the commons in the
neighbourhood of the metropolis have not yet
been destroyed. A considerable tract still remains. Let us hope that a warning has been
given in time, and that the government will never
again be permitted to barter away, for an insignificant sum, which would be wasted in one useless military experiment, proprietary rights which
have a value beyond price, not only to countless
thousands who are now living, but which may
be still more precious to the millions who in
future ages are destined to uphold the industrial
fabric of this nation.

Whilst we are considering the vital importance of obtaining open spaces of ground as public property in the neighbourhood of large towns, we are naturally led to notice another aspect of the land question. It is one which suggests topics of grave and pressing significance. It can be scarcely necessary to remark to you that the land on which a city is built, must rapidly become more valuable, as its population and wealth increase. London may now be regarded as the great emporium of the world's commerce. History furnishes no parallel of such an accumulation of wealth, and this wealth seems to be so distributed that the rich grow rapidly richer, whilst there is no perceptible advance in the comfort enjoyed by the industrial classes. I do not of course deny that money wages have been augmented by this increase of capital, but this apparent advantage is to a great extent lost, because many of the necessaries of life are becoming dearer. The great difficulty with which the labourers in our large towns have to contend is the scarcity of house-accommodation; moreover this is a difficulty which is to a great extent created by our material prosperity, and it is one which grows with the growth of wealth; for what is the spectacle which London presents at the present time? Land is there becoming too valuable, either for the erection, or the retention of humble dwellings. The homes of the poor are being rapidly swept away, in order to make room for offices, shops, warehouses, and all the other appliances of increasing commerce. The suburbs of the metropolis are being covered with the villa residences of the wealthy, and thousands of labourers' houses have been destroyed by the railways which now intersect London, and which are absolutely required in order to circulate the augmented traffic. You will readily understand the sad consequences which ensue. A greater number of human beings have to find accommodation in a smaller number of houses; overcrowding with all its attendant evils is inevitable, the comfort of the poor is diminished, morality cannot thrive when people are compelled to huddle together regardless of every decency of life ; all the conditions upon which health depends are ignored, and typhus and other diseases assume the constancy of an epidemic. But you will perhaps ask whether an efficient remedy can be suggested. I cannot hope that any remedy will be completely effectual ; I do however maintain that where such evils are more or less the natural accompaniments of our present commercial development, they should, as far as possible, be counteracted, and not encouraged by our legislature.

It is evident that what is wanted, is land upon

which dwellings for the industrial classes could be
erected. I do not advocate any undue Government
interference, but I think that the remarks which
have been made upon this subject supply not the
least forcible arguments in favour of those altera-
tions in the law of real property, which would, as
we have shewn, facilitate the acquisition of land.
Natural causes are each year tending to make land
in the neighbourhood of our large towns more and
more scarce; let not therefore this scarcity be promoted by laws which prevent land being brought
into the market, and which also augment the
cost of transferring land from one proprietor to
another. It is more than probable that the difficulty of supplying house-accommodation for the
poor will become so great that some other legislative interference will be needed. The industrial
classes will each year be compelled to live at a
greater distance from their work, and the question
will therefore arise, whether the Government ought
not to compel the metropolitan railways to run
special cheap trains for the convenience of working
men. At the suggestion of Lord Derby, a standing
order has been passed, which will secure that these
cheap trains should be run on each new railway
which is brought into London. Let us hope that
the same provision will be extended to all the
existing metropolitan railways. No one can fairly

say that the rights of private property will be thus unduly interfered with; for when permission to make a particular railway is granted, a monopoly is conferred upon the proprietors of the railway, and the legislature has an indisputable right to make those who accept and enjoy a monopoly, use it in such a way as will most effectually promote the well-being of the country.

CHAPTER III.

Cooperation.

IN the last chapter an incidental allusion was made to the industrial projects which have been, and may be carried on by associations of labourers. Our national economy is at the present time characterised by a complete separation between capital and labour. One class, termed employers, supply the capital which industry requires, and another class, who are the employed, supply the requisite labour. The proceeds of industry are divided into two distinct shares; the one share is the wages which the labourer receives as his remuneration, and the other share is given to the capitalist in the form of profits; these profits reward him for the investment of his capital and for his labour of superintendence. It is evident, however, that the labourer will enjoy the whole proceeds of his industry, or in other words, that profits as well as wages will be allotted to him, if he, instead of obtaining a supply of capital from another, provides all the capital which his labour may require. Thus the peasant proprietor owns the land which he cultivates, and also furnishes the necessary capital, and consequently the whole produce yielded becomes his property. Formerly the artisan capitalists who worked on their own account, and not for a master, were a numerous class: but many of the causes which have swept away the small freeholders of bygone days, have also operated to destroy those domestic manufactures which once represented so large a portion of the industry of this country.

I have already shewn, that as the implements of agriculture have been improved, farming on a large scale has become more profitable. For similar reasons the handloom weavers, the pillow lace-makers, and many others who once carried on manufactures in their own homes, were inevitably destined to succumb to the new order of things which was created by such modern inventions as those which were achieved by the genius of Arkwright and Watt. When lace was made on a pillow, and when woollen and cotton cloth were woven by hand, manufactures could be carried on in the houses of the labourers. Then no advantage resulted from collecting a great number of operatives under one roof. The present, however, is peculiarly an age for production on a large scale; manufactories are increasing in size; their machinery is becoming more extensive and costly, and within certain limits the rate of profits realized from a business seems to augment as the scale upon which the business is conducted is increased. Many of those who have been most successful in commerce have not unfrequently a capital of £100,000 invested in their industrial occupations. It would therefore seem that all the tendencies of modern times combine to make it more impossible for the artisan to become his own master, and thus advance himself beyond the position of a hired labourer. Suppose, for instance, that a cotton operative should by great prudence and self-denial save £200. With such an amount of capital it would be absurd of him to think of commencing manufacturing cotton on his own account; he might of course undertake some small business, say, a retail shop, but he would then be embarking in a business which he did not understand, and all that wonderful skill which has only been acquired by the training of years would be of no further use to him. But suppose there are 250 operatives, who, like the one we have been describing, have saved £200; they agree to unite their joint savings in a common fund. A capital of £50,000 would thus be created; this amount would be amply sufficient to enable them to become the proprietors of a cotton-mill, as large as any of those in which the greatest profits have been realized. These 250 operatives might further agree to supply the labour which this mill required. Hence they would provide both capital and labour. The whole proceeds of their industry would be their own property; wages and profits would be merged in the aggregate remuneration which they received, instead of being allotted to reward two distinct classes, viz. the employers and employed. A complete union of capital and labour would thus be established, and this union has been termed Co-operation.

I purpose to describe to you the various phases through which Cooperation has passed. I shall shew you that many of the schemes which are known as cooperative, only deserve the appellation in a modified sense. I shall endeavour to compare the benefits which will result from co-operation, with the disadvantages and difficulties which may impede its progress. This union of capital and labour was first crudely suggested by the earliest and most distinguished Socialists and Communists, amongst whom may be ranked Fourier, St Simon, and our countryman, Owen. These men are too frequently despised, because their particular schemes have not been practically successful. Let us, however, do justice to their memory. They were no doubt visionary and enthusiastic, but they were men who were eminently good and noble; their lives moreover were not spent in vain. They were the first to recognise the evils which are associated with our present industrial economy. They perceived that so far as the production of wealth was concerned, society was tending to separate itself into classes which were kept apart by the rivalry of self-interest, and they therefore sought to establish communities where there should be no antagonism between capital and labour, but where all should feel that they were working for the common good. I need not stay to describe to you the details connected with the inevitable failure of such schemes; I should not have referred to them, did I not feel that if I passed them by unnoticed, I should have done injustice to the memory of the earlier Socialists: for amongst those who joined these ill-fated communistic schemes, there were some who obtained an invaluable experience, which has enabled them to become the originators of the Cooperative movement.

Many of the earlier disciples of Communism, although they had to witness the failure of their schemes, yet became permanently impressed with the advantages which working men would obtain by uniting for a common object. The first attempts which were thus made to cooperate were rude and simple; but although the commencement was imperfect and unpretending, yet a great social and economic movement was commenced.   Already great results have been achieved, although cooperation may be regarded as being yet in the infancy of its development.   So much is this the case in our own country, that scarcely any of the societies which are termed cooperative deserve the title; for up to the present time the principle has been almost entirely applied to the distribution, and not to the production of wealth.   Thus the most extensive and most prosperous Cooperative establishment in England is the celebrated Rochdale Pioneers' Society.   But this society ought to be regarded as a Store, from which produce is distributed; and in this case, it cannot be said that labourers combine their capital in order to produce wealth. I will however briefly describe the progress of this remarkable Society.   Its history possesses singular interest, and I shall then be able to make you more clearly perceive the difference between a cooperative store and a cooperative trading establishment. This distinction, although generally ignored, is still very important.

In 1844, twenty-eight poor Rochdale weavers appeared to be impressed with the conviction, that their lot might be improved if they adopted some united action. They had seen that generation after generation of working men had supported various schemes which had ended, either in disaster or in disappointment. Communism had failed as a practical measure, and those who had joined a popular agitation for a new political charter had received no adequate compensation for the self-sacrifice which they were often compelled to endure. These poor Rochdale weavers were shrewd and intelligent. After they had calmly reflected upon the various modes which had been propounded for improving the lot of the labourer, they calmly arrived at the conclusion that they had little chance of immediately increasing their income, although it was easily within their power to economise their expenditure. They knew that they purchased the commodities which they consumed at a price which greatly exceeded the wholesale price; moreover adulteration was not unfrequently resorted to; and thus it often happened that the articles which the labourer purchased were not only dear, but also impure. These weavers therefore determined to create a sufficient sum by weekly contributions to enable them to purchase, on the same terms as the wholesale trader, a few simple commodities, such as tea and sugar. In the first instance each of these twenty-eight weavers agreed to give twopence a week to the common fund. They were so poor

that it was not without a struggle that this weekly
contribution was raised to threepence a week.   At
length the amount thus collected somewhat exceeded £20, and trading operations were commenced.   A room was taken as a store in Toad
Lane; this store was in the first instance opened
only for a few hours during one day in the week.
At the outset some preliminary difficulties were
encountered; thus a few of the subscribers who
lived at a distance from the store found some in-
convenience in dealing there, and consequently the
amount of business transacted was not quite so
great as anticipated.   But the sound and admirable
principles which regulated the management of the
concern soon caused every obstacle to be surmounted, and this humble society in a few years
advanced with sure and steady steps to the most
extraordinary prosperity.   At the close of 1845
the Society numbered eighty members, its capital
was £182, and its weekly sales averaged £30.   In
1847—48, the cotton-trade was greatly depressed,
and severe distress prevailed amongst the operatives.   It might have been reasonably anticipated
that necessity would have compelled the working
men to withdraw their capital from this Pioneers'
Society, but these forebodings were not realized;
the difficulties were weathered so triumphantly,
that from that time the permanent prosperity of

the society might be regarded as insured. As distress pressed upon the operatives, they were more and more desirous to economise their reduced wages, and they consequently enrolled themselves as members of the society. The result was, that at the end of 1848 the members had increased to 140 in number, the capital was £397, and the weekly receipts were £180. The progress from this time was rapid. In 1850 the number of members amounted to 600, they possessed a capital of £2299, and their weekly returns were £338. Each year seemed to bring continually increasing prosperity. The society has grown into a vast commercial concern; for at the present time (the close of 1864) its capital is £62,000, its annual business amounts to £174,900; the annual profits are £22,700, and its members number 4747.

The humble room where the enterprise was first started has now grown into a large warehouse, to which are affiliated sixteen branch stores. At first grocery was alone sold; now the working man can purchase from this store every article of food and clothing which he may require. They not only have butchers' shops, but they make shoes, and almost every article of wearing apparel. They have also erected steam-flour-mills, and they are thus enabled to be their own millers and bakers. But the benefits which this society has conferred

upon the working man are not confined to mere
pecuniary gains, for he has had brought within his
reach social and educational advantages, which he
could never have obtained without such an union
of effort. Two and a half per cent of the aggregate
profits realised are set aside to support a reading-
room and a library. The library consists of 4000
volumes, and has been admirably selected; not
only the members of the Society, but also their
wives and families, are freely admitted to the reading-room, which is well warmed, and furnished
with a bountiful·supply of newspapers, reviews, and
maps. It thus appears that pecuniary profit con-
stitutes only a portion of the advantage which may
be derived from such institutions as the one we
have been describing. The working men who thus
combine soon become united to each other by
many social bonds. In this reading-room they
enjoy the pleasures of conversation and society.
They occasionally arrange amongst themselves ex-
cursions into the country; microscopes and other
scientific instruments are provided by the society
for those who may happen to have a taste for
natural science. When men are thus brought together they lose much of that selfishness which is
sure to be engendered in those who never leave the
domestic circle. The Rochdale Pioneers have frequently shewn that they possess a generous pa-

triotism, for when a public object deserves their support, they have again and again proved that they are ready to assist it with a handsome subscription.

It may perhaps be thought that this society, starting from so humble a commencement, could have never achieved such great results, if it had not been assisted by some exceptionally favourable circumstances. We will therefore investigate the principles of management which were adopted, and then we shall be able more fairly to conclude whether similar schemes would in other localities obtain corresponding success. The Rochdale Pioneers have always strictly observed the rule, that no credit should be either given or taken, they both buy and sell their goods for ready money. Even a shareholder cannot make the smallest purchase without paying for it across the counter. It would be almost impossible to exaggerate the advantages which have been secured by strictly adhering to this ready money principle. For instance, no bad debt can ever be made, and thus one important item of serious loss is avoided. Since ready money is always paid, the goods which the society purchases can be bought on the most favourable terms. Again, when no credit is given, there is no money locked up in book debts, and a very large business can be done with a

6

comparatively small capital; the permanent stability of the society is thus secured, for if its business should suffer from distress amongst the operatives of the district, its trade operations could be contracted without loss, when there are no outstanding credit obligations. The working men who are thus encouraged to make their purchases for ready money, are emancipated from one of the chief dangers which threaten their welfare and prosperity. The facility with which credit is given has caused the ruin of many thousands of labourers. They perhaps in the first instance begin by getting into debt for a small amount; they become almost the slaves of the tradesman to whom they owe money; they are no longer free to deal where they like, and they are often compelled to pay a high price for very inferior articles. The labourer becomes gradually more and more involved. As his difficulties accumulate, his recklessness increases; at last he perhaps resorts to the public-house, in the hope that he may there forget his misery, and lose sight of his impending ruin.

After the Pioneers had agreed neither to give nor to receive credit, they next directed their attention to the principles which should regulate the distribution of profits. The plan which was adopted was most wisely conceived. It was decided that the first charge upon the profits should be a fixed dividend of 5 per cent. on the capital, and the remaining profits were divided amongst the shareholders, in proportion to the amount of their purchases. The register of these purchases is kept in a very ingenious manner. Each customer when paying for his goods, receives some tin tickets or tallies, which record the amount he has expended. At the end of each quarter he brings these tickets, which are the registers of his aggregate purchases, and which show the portion of the profits due to him. The drawback thus given on the amount of money expended has often amounted to 1*s*. 3*d*. in the £. Many of the shareholders leave their portion of the profits as capital in the society, and in some cases very considerable sums have thus been accumulated.

I think that this brief sketch of the Rochdale Pioneers will convince you that from such societies the working men may derive inestimable advantages. I should however be sorry to conceal from you the fact that many similar institutions have been established, and that the same success has not always been obtained. To take a striking example, it may be said that these societies have to a great extent failed in London. Let us inquire why a trading institution which is so eminently prosperous in Rochdale, should wither and fade in the metropolis. This inquiry will be moreover

instructive, because it will show us the real nature
of these societies, which I think have been erroneously called cooperative. For instance, I believe
that the Rochdale Pioneers' Society ought properly to be regarded as a Joint-Stock Company.
A number of individuals, not necessarily working
men, subscribe a certain sum as capital for the
purpose of trading. The business is conducted by
paid managers and other paid servants. Such an
establishment is therefore a joint-stock company,
created by uniting the small capitals of the poor;
the company is not one of production, but it fulfils
the functions of distribution, which are carried on
by the retail trader. In a business which simply
consists of distribution, there cannot be that union
of capital and labour which in my opinion consti-
tutes the essence of cooperation.

As we have now ascertained the real nature of
the societies which are termed cooperative stores,
we shall be able more accurately to estimate the
causes which may on the one hand assist, and on
the other hand, retard the progress of such institutions. The father of Economic Science, Adam
Smith, has propounded an exhaustive analysis of
the advantages and disadvantages, which are associated with the joint-stock principle. He rightly
concludes that the paid manager of a company is
seldom likely to be so efficient a man of business

as the individual trader, who is constantly prompted to activity and energy by the powerful feeling of self-interest. Experience has consequently shown, that a business which requires constant watchfulness and an unflagging attention to minute details is not likely to be carried on successfully by a joint-stock company. It might appear that the retail trades which are embraced in the dealings of a cooperative store, belong to that particular class of business which is peculiarly unsuited to a joint-stock company. It might therefore seem that these cooperative institutions unless aided by special circumstances would be unable to compete with retail traders. This conclusion is strikingly corroborated by facts, for the cooperative stores have prospered in those towns where they have been assisted by favourable circumstances, and they have failed in those localities, where these favourable circumstances have been unable to operate. As an example, let us consider how different is the position of one of these stores in Rochdale, and one in London.

The success of the Rochdale Pioneers' Society is no doubt due to the following causes:—First, no credit is given. Secondly, the society has been managed by men of rare business qualifications, and implicit confidence has been most wisely reposed in these managers. Thirdly, the shareholders of the Society constitute a body of customers, who will deal at the Store without being specially attracted to it. Hence no expense for advertisements need be incurred, no costly shop-fronts are required; the business need not be carried on in crowded thoroughfares, where rents are high; its appropriate situation being in the centre of the locality where the labourers reside.

There is obviously no reason why the first and second of these advantages should not be secured by any cooperative Store wherever it may be situated. It is at least not too much to say that they are essential elements of success. If these societies either give or receive credit, their failure is inevitable. Again, failure would be equally certain, if the shareholders of the society have not the wisdom to appoint as managers those who are best qualified. It will be perceived that the last of the three classes of advantages which have been enumerated, is in a certain degree dependent on locality. Rochdale is, comparatively speaking, a small town, and the shareholders of the Pioneers' Society are not so widely scattered as to make it inconvenient for them to deal at the Store. But in London the members of a similar society would probably live several miles distant from each other, and consequently when the Store was started, a considerable portion of the shareholders would live at too great a distance to deal with it. Hence, in London, it is probable that such a society, at its first commencement would not have a sufficient number of customers. Of course it may be said that many would soon become customers who were not shareholders of the society. But if it was thus necessary to rely upon the general public, the co-operative Store would immediately be brought into direct competition with the retail shops, and those expenses would have to be incurred which are resorted to with the view of attracting purchasers. Experience has proved, as might have been anticipated, that in such a competition the retail shops are likely to prove successful. Hence in large towns it would be advisable to commence a co-operative Store, on so comparatively small a scale, that the majority of those who join it may live in the same neighbourhood. The difficulty of securing customers would in this way be obviated. An humble commencement need be no cause for discouragement; it should always be remembered that the Rochdale Pioneers began with a weekly subscription of twopence from twenty-eight members. Perhaps the most satisfactory feature connected with these institutions is, that the scale on which they are conducted does not apparently affect either the success they obtain, or the advantages which they confer. In many villages co-

operative Stores have been established, and have
prospered greatly.

It may perhaps be thought that I should have
given more encouragement to cooperation, if I
had not laid so much stress upon the fact that
these Stores are ordinary Joint-Stock Companies.
I have however had a distinct purpose in view. I
feared that some might think that associated with
cooperation, there was some special virtue which
would at once dissipate the difficulties which beset
the path of ordinary industry. It therefore becomes most important not in the least degree to
disguise the real nature of these societies; they,
like other joint-stock companies will succeed, if
managers can be secured, who will be as active,
intelligent, and watchful, as individual traders. But
these societies will inevitably fail if bad debts are
permitted to absorb profits, or if the general body
of the shareholders should so much interfere with
those who manage the business, that their energy is
hampered, and their superior judgment and knowledge over-ruled. It has now however been conclusively proved, that in a vast number of towns
and villages these cooperative Stores have succeeded most admirably, and working men have
therefore now abundant experience, from which
they may obtain not only encouragement, but also
guidance and instruction. They, if they like to

make the inquiry, will be emphatically told by those who have become members of such a society as the Rochdale Pioneers, that these institutions give the labourers an opportunity of self-help; and if they really wish to improve their condition, they must chiefly rely upon their own efforts, and not upon the favour or kindness of others.

A moment's reflection will show how great is the influence exerted by a Cooperative Store. In the first place, it affords the labourers an eligible investment for their capital. Improvidence has hitherto been the great bane of our industrial classes. Nothing however has so much tended to foster this vice, as the difficulty of obtaining an eligible investment for small sums of money. The Savings-Banks have been admirable institutions, and the country owes a debt of gratitude to the present Chancellor of the Exchequer for having given the poor an opportunity of depositing their savings, with all the security which the credit of the State can give. But when money is thus invested, the interest obtained is only about $2\frac{1}{2}$ per cent., and this small return frequently does not act as a sufficiently powerful motive to induce prudence. In contrast with such an indifferent investment, the Rochdale Pioneers obtain a fixed dividend of 5 per cent. on their capital, and in addition, they receive a drawback on their purchases, which

frequently amounts to 1s. 3d. in the £. But this
difference in the aggregate return to their capital, great as it may be, is not the most striking
feature of the contrast. The working man who
has £50 deposited in a Post Office Savings-Bank
receives his half-yearly dividend, which amounts to
12s. 6d., with the strictest punctuality; he however
derives no other advantage from the investment.
The working man who has £50 invested with the
Rochdale Pioneers, has hitherto received much
larger dividends with equal regularity, but the
benefits which he derives from this investment are
by no means confined to pecuniary profits; he becomes a member of an agreeable artisans' club; he
and his family have the use of an excellent reading-room and library; he is thrown into pleasing
social relationship with many of his fellow-la-
bourers. A sympathy, a brotherly kindness, and a
generosity of spirit are thus engendered, which by
elevating the mind and character, give to life its
greatest happiness. The working men also thus
receive a training and education which may be invaluable to them in after life; they have to exercise
discrimination in selecting the best men as the
managers of the society, and they have to show
forbearance and firmness in obeying and upholding
the authority of those who are appointed to manage
their affairs. These are the qualities which must

be possessed by our industrial classes, if they are ever to be raised above the condition of labourers working for hire.

The truth of this last remark will be amply verified, as we proceed to consider the consequences which result from cooperation, when it is applied not simply to the distribution, but also to the production of wealth. It has already been stated, that the store whose progress and prospects we have been describing, cannot rightly be called cooperative, for this word implies an union between capital and labour. If, for instance, the labourers who work in a cotton-mill, own all the capital embarked in the business, it is obvious that in this case there will be a complete union between capital and labour, and the manufactory will be conducted on pure cooperative principles. Although institutions of this kind are extremely rare in England, yet in France many have been carried on with remarkable success. So far as our own country is concerned, Rochdale seems to be the centre of all the various phases of the cooperative movement. The leading members of the Pioneers' Society were so encouraged by their success, that they were naturally induced to extend the principle of union, and they resolved to unite their capitals, in order to commence trading on their own account. They perceived that in this way the whole fruits of their industry would become their own. The promoters of the scheme were chiefly cotton-operatives, and they therefore resolved to continue the business to which they had been accustomed. The experiment was commenced very cautiously. It was determined in 1855 to begin the scheme by renting a shed, which contained a certain number of spindles and other requisite machinery. The success immediately obtained was so great, that the scheme was rapidly extended. The humble shed was soon relinquished, and it was determined to rent a portion of a mill. The capital at that time possessed by the society amounted to £5000. The principles of management were most wisely conceived; those who laboured were paid the wages current in the district, and the profits were divided according to the following plan:—A dividend of 5 per cent. on the capital invested was the first charge upon profits, and after this charge had been liquidated, one half of the remaining profits was given as an extra dividend on capital, and the remaining half was given as a bonus to labour, each operative's share of this bonus being in proportion to the aggregate amount of wages which he had received. The annual profits realised were on the average about $13\frac{1}{2}$ per cent., and the profits distributed amongst the labourers amounted to a very considerable sum. Such prosperity naturally inspired the greatest

confidence, and consequently it was soon resolved
to be in no way dependent on others; it was therefore determined to erect a mill. The foundation
stone of this building was laid in 1856. The operatives of the district felt such confidence in the
undertaking that many eagerly subscribed all the
money which they either possessed or could save;
and the supply of capital was so abundant, that the
mill was completed in about three years; it was
filled with the best machinery; its whole cost was
£45,000; and competent authorities have unanimously affirmed, that there is not a better or more
complete mill in the district. After the building
and machinery had been paid for, the capital which
was left, was amply sufficient to carry on a large
and enterprising business. Just at the time when
this cooperative manufactory was completed, the
American Civil War began; we were deprived of
our chief supply of raw cotton, and the cotton trade
was prostrated. The scheme therefore has as yet
had no chance of achieving the full extent of its
possible success. The trials which it has had to
bear throughout this period of unparalleled adversity, have been so triumphantly surmounted, as to
justify a confident belief in the future of such undertakings. Whilst the American Civil War continued, the industry of Lancashire was paralysed;
few indeed of the wealthiest manufacturers could

work their mills whole time, and many were obliged to close their mills altogether. Tens of thousands of operatives were thrown out of employment; they were too independent to ask for alms until they were compelled to do so by dire necessity. When assistance had to be sought, even the charity of a generous and wealthy nation was insufficient, and the State was obliged to supply relief. But throughout this melancholy period, the Rochdale Cooperative Mill struggled on manfully; it could not have borne up more bravely against the difficulties of the times, even if it had been backed by the capital of a millionnaire. With the exception of about four or five months, the mill has kept working full time; the operatives employed in it have been paid their wages with the utmost regularity; and during the crisis, the dividend on capital was on the average about 5 per cent. The whole capital now embarked in this undertaking is £92,000. Even in the darkest days of this gloomy period, so little were the operatives discouraged, that a second mill was commenced and rapidly completed.

But whilst congratulating the working men on this splendid achievement, I cannot help feeling great regret that the principles upon which this undertaking was commenced, have been materially changed. I have already told you that it was at first wisely decided, that profits should be distributed between capital and labour. About three years since, this method of distribution was altered, and it was then resolved, that henceforth labour should not participate in the profits. The society has thus lost its cooperative character; it is now an ordinary joint-stock company; a portion of whose capital happens to be owned by those who are employed as labourers in the concern.

I think however that this departure from the principle of cooperation ought to cause neither surprise nor discouragement; for let us for a moment consider the position in which the shareholders of this cotton-mill were placed, and we shall then be able to estimate the seductive power of the temptation, which they were called upon to resist. It must be borne in mind that many of the operatives employed at this mill had no capital invested in the Company; moreover, a considerable portion of the capital was owned by those who had been trained to other branches of industry; and who would of course never seek employment in a cotton mill. These particular shareholders would very naturally say, In no manufactory in the country are higher wages paid than in ours; in none is employment more regular; and no similar building can be better ventilated, and in every respect more comfortable. Operatives therefore will most gladly work for us, if they simply receive the current rate

of wages; why therefore should we distribute annually amongst them many hundreds, or perhaps
thousands, as an additional gratuity for which we
get no return? The most wealthy manufacturers
never perform such acts of generosity; the money
thus voluntarily appropriated is our own property;
we have every right to enjoy it; and it would materially increase the returns yielded to the capital,
which we were unable to save without great self-
sacrifice. It is not surprising, that influenced by
such arguments as these, a considerable majority
of the share-holders were induced to pass a resolution, which declared that labour should not participate in the profits realised. A minority sternly
opposed the resolution, and have since made many
fruitless attempts to rescind it. In this minority
there were many who were early members of the
Pioneers' Society; these men were so devoted to
the cooperative principle, that they would willingly
make some sacrifice on its behalf; they were men
whose training had made them prudent and intelligent, and they could recognise the occasions
when prospective advantage demanded the relin-
quishment of some present profit.

This minority forcibly argued that the chief
guarantee for the permanent prosperity of their
manufactory would be destroyed, if the labourer
was permitted to enjoy no share of the profits rea-

lised. A cooperative establishment in common with all joint-stock undertakings, has to encounter some disadvantages which do not to the same extent affect a business which is conducted by an individual capitalist. For instance, as I have already said, it can scarcely be expected that a paid manager will be so energetic, and in every respect so efficient, as the owner of a business, whose activity and zeal are constantly stimulated by so powerful an incentive, as self-interest. But this disadvantage is far more than counterbalanced, if a joint-stock company is carried on upon the cooperative principle; for if labourers are permitted to participate in the profits, they at once become interested in the prosperity of the business, they are consequently prompted to exert themselves to the utmost, and hence, as has well been said, cooperation will attract the most efficient labourers, and will secure their best and most skilled efforts. In this way, the most glaring defect in our present industrial economy will be remedied, and we may be sure that labour cannot be efficient, and industry cannot permanently thrive, if employers and employed do not become more united by some of the feelings which result from common pecuniary interest.

These considerations induce me to agree with those who think that the Rochdale Cooperative Cotton Company, in thus departing from the cooperative principle lost one great element of success; yet, in spite of this, its present wonderful prosperity has been achieved. I therefore think that this society affords the most gratifying and conclusive evidence, that associations of labourers can successfully carry on trading operations, even when they simply constitute themselves into an ordinary joint-stock company. How much more confident of success may we feel, when the advantage of making these associations cooperative shall be fully recognised! Perhaps it will be thought that in selecting this Rochdale Manufactory, I have taken an exceptionally favourable case. I should be sorry to ignore a single case of failure, but I have been obliged to describe the Rochdale Mill in some detail, because, in England, it is the only instance in which labourers have combined on so large a scale with the view of trading on their own account. In several branches of industry, where production is naturally on a small scale, associations of labourers have been successfully formed. Thus, in Manchester, there is a cooperative society for making hats, and in London, there is one for making picture-frames. If, however, we desire to obtain the fullest information on the subject, we must turn to France; for in that country, there are many associations of labourers which carry on trade upon pure cooperative principles.

Socialism and Communism made a much deeper impression upon the French nation than upon our own people. The French have been so much accustomed to dwell on these theories, that the working men of that country believed, that their condition could only be improved, and society could only be regenerated, by introducing different economic relations between capital and labour. When therefore the revolution of 1848 dethroned the monarch, and placed supreme power in the hands of the people, the popular leaders who formed the Provisional Government, directed more attention to the formation of social schemes, than to the construction of a new political constitution. Although the schemes which were thus started were ill conceived and mischievous in their tendencies, yet it was intended that the same objects should be attained as are supposed to be accomplished by cooperation. Louis Blanc, who might be regarded as representing the social economy element in the Provisional Government, has always undoubtedly been a sincere, yet mistaken friend of cooperation. He determined to carry the principle into practical effect by calling in the assistance of the State; he wished to make the labourers enjoy the whole fruits of their industry; he saw that they could not do so, unless they became possessors of capital; Louis Blanc seemed to forget that capital was the

result of saving; possibly too, his benevolent heart
shrank from asking the poor to save; and perhaps
too, he thought that even if they did save, it would
be so slow a process, as too long to delay the social
regeneration which he so eagerly anticipated.   He
therefore resolved, that associations of labourers
should be permitted to borrow from the State sufficient capital, to enable them to commence business
on their own account.   Hence national workshops
were established.   A more mischievous scheme was
never conceived; it was essentially unjust; the
capital which was thus lent to workmen, had of
course to be procured by taxation, and this taxation was imposed upon the general community,
many of whom would be thus compulsorily obliged
to give pecuniary support to schemes which would
inflict the most direct injury upon them; for it is
evident that employers of labour would be injured,
if those whom they employed were attracted to
these national workshops.   The injustice was not of
long continuance; for, as might have been anticipated, the whole affair proved a disastrous failure.
Immediately this State assistance was granted, the
labourers lost their self-dependence; the unfortunate opinion was impressed upon them that they
need not rely upon their own efforts now that
the maintenance of their prosperity was recognised as the first duty of the Government.   When

Louis Napoleon gained supreme power, and made the people and the institutions of France obey his individual will, these national workshops were swept away, because it was thought that they might become dangerous political organizations. But even if they had been left undisturbed, they could not have long survived. A social structure raised upon a basis of economic delusions and fallacies was soon destined to totter and fall, and its ruins would serve as sad, yet instructive memorials of the disasters which result from unwise and misdirected government interference.

Whilst inevitable misfortune was impending over these State Societies, some Parisian workmen were associating, determined to rely entirely upon their own efforts. The very difficulties which, in the beginning they had to encounter, gave them an experience, which ensured future success. The Parisian workmen when forming these associations usually adopted a rule, which made it more easy strictly to adhere to the cooperative principle; for in most cases it was decided, that none but shareholders should be employed as labourers. The adoption of this rule to a great extent obviated the difficulty which has so much tended to thwart the efficiency of the Rochdale Cooperative Manufactory; for if all the labourers employed are shareholders, the hostility which is supposed to exist between capital and labour would be greatly weakened; these two interests would be more united, and there would then be little chance that labour would be refused all participation in the profits realised.   Moreover, when the labourers have capital in the business, no very great evil would result from appropriating all the profits to capital.   The great industrial advantage of coopera-ration would still operate, since all the labouring shareholders would be directly interested in the prosperity of the business.   The cooperative trad-ing societies in Paris are very numerous.   I will proceed to describe the progress of one or two of them, and the details of their prosperity will prove to you, that a way has now been discovered by which a labourer may raise his own condition, and may make his life what it has never been before.

In the year 1852, seventeen Parisian masons determined to form themselves into a cooperative society; they had then a capital of only £14. 10s., which they had accumulated by saving one-tenth of their daily earnings.   At the end of the year 1854, the capital had increased to £680; and in 1860 the society consisted of 107 members, and the capital possessed by them was £14,500.   The fol-lowing are some of the important buildings which have been erected in Paris by this society:—The Hôtel Fould, in the rue de Berry; the Hôtel Rouher, in the Champs Elysées; the Hôtel Frescati, rue de Richelieu; the Square d'Orleans, rue Tait-bout, etc.: and lately these cooperative masons were building an hôtel for M. Girardin, on the Boulevard of the king of Rome; an hôtel for M. Arsénne Haussage, on the Boulevard de l'Empereur; and an hôtel at Montrouge for M. Pacotte. The labourers are paid the ordinary wages current in the trade, and the nett profits realised are apportioned in the following manner:—Two-fifths of these profits form a fund, from which the annual dividend on capital is paid; and the remaining three-fifths are appropriated to provide an extra bonus on labour. The bonus which each labourer thus receives, is proportioned to the amount of labour he has performed throughout the year. No arrangements that could be devised would more powerfully promote the efficiency of labour. This is the secret of the remarkable success of this society. The cooperative masons have fairly entered into the great field of commercial competition; they have striven to do their work cheaper and better than others; and it is because they have proved that they can work cheaper and better, that they have been employed to build residences for such persons as M. Girardin, and the others we have enumerated.

The next Parisian Society which we shall describe is also one which, in its infancy, had to struggle against most formidable difficulties. In 1848, fourteen pianoforte makers resolved to form themselves into an association; they were as poor as men could be; they had no capital, and scarcely any tools, and they were also refused any loan from the State. After bravely enduring the most severe hardships, they succeeded in saving £45, and with this they determined to commence business. They at first rented a very small room in an obscure part of Paris. Fortunately a timber merchant was so much impressed in their favour, that he was induced to give them some credit. For many months they denied themselves every luxury; in fact it was impossible to have lived on more scanty or frugal fare. One incident will illustrate the difficulty of their position. They joyfully accepted an offer from a baker to purchase a piano for £19, and to pay them for it in bread. This bread was for a considerable time the chief means of their support. All obstacles were however one by one surmounted, and their progress, though gradual, was steady and sure. In 1850, the members of the society increased to 32; they had left their first humble room, and were now renting a commodious building at £80 a year; at this time their stock was worth £1600. Within the last few years they have become the owners of a large freehold manufactory, which is furnished with the most improved machinery, and the business which they now annually transact exceeds £8000. This Pianoforte Association has obtained a well-deserved reputation for the excellence and cheapness of its work.

Other examples might be enumerated, with the view of showing the rapid growth of cooperative societies in Germany and various continental countries. I think however, that from the facts which have been adduced, you will be able to understand the real nature of this new social and economic movement. The instances which have been brought forward, clearly demonstrate that the poorest artizans, by forming themselves into Associations, may raise themselves above the position of hired labourers and become successful traders. I do not however disguise from myself the fact that these associations require from the labourer many virtues and qualifications, which are perhaps unfortunately to be regarded as rare endowments. He must be thrifty and prudent; he must have the courage to bear at the outset many sufferings; he must have the discrimination to select the best men to be managers of the association; and he must without cavil obey those whom he has placed in this position of responsibility. He must moreover accept the lessons of experience, and thus learn when trade is good to set aside a portion of the profits, in order to tide over the depression of bad times. It may in fact be briefly said that the members of prosperous cooperative societies are men who possess a character which entitles them to be considered the élite of the labouring population. No one therefore who is acquainted with our own country, can suppose that the majority of our working classes could immediately establish cooperative societies with a fair chance of success. I should be the last to make this statement with any feeling of reproach against those who live by daily toil; for when we reflect upon the circumstances which too often surround the youth and the manhood of our labourers, we need not be disheartened because intemperance and improvidence are frequent. If there is crime, we must remember that a considerable number of the humbler classes of this country are uneducated, and statistics have indisputably demonstrated, that ignorance and crime are inseparably associated*. If drunkenness abounds, we must not forget that the public-house will always prove attractive, if the labourers' dwellings are too miserable to afford any of the comforts of a home. If many working men are reckless with regard to

* The Judicial Statistics of 1863, show that out of 129,527 persons committed to prison in England and Wales during that year, only 4829 could read and write well.

the future, we must recollect, that unless the mind is trained, man will always be powerfully influenced by mere animal instincts; self-indulgence becomes his controlling passion, and if the intellect remains dormant, a prudent foresight with regard to the future, will rarely act with sufficient force to induce the sacrifice of any temporary enjoyment.

When therefore we consider the present condition of our labourers, I think we must conclude that as they step by step improve, cooperation and other systems of industrial economy, superior to those which now exist, will be gradually introduced. Before any considerable portion of the trade of this country can be conducted on the cooperative principle, I believe that the labourers must be trained and educated for this new state of things, by passing through several transitional economic phases. Thus it seems probable from many events which have recently occurred, that a very general introduction of what has been termed copartnership, may be one of the first changes in our national industry. A copartnership is said to exist, when an employer agrees to distribute a portion of his profits amongst those whom he employs. I shall hereafter show that whenever this system has been tried, it has proved most beneficial both to masters and men. Unfor-

tunate disputes, such as strikes, which so greatly
impede the prosperity of trade, are thus effectually
obviated; the employed become directly interested
in the success of the work in which they are engaged; their zeal and activity are stimulated; hence
their labour becomes so much more efficient, that
the employer is abundantly recompensed for the
portion of his profits which he agrees to relinquish.

The two systems of copartnership and cooperation are very happily blended in some of our large
commercial concerns, when they are converted into
joint-stock companies. The owners of the business
become directors of the company, and retain a
large portion, say two-thirds of the capital. The
shares, which represent the remainder of the capital, are first offered to those who are employed in
the establishment, and the working men who take
up these shares are permitted to choose two or
three directors; this arrangement enables every
labourer to become in part a proprietor of the
business or trade in which he works. Capital and
labour thus become to a great extent united; the
working men, when called upon to elect directors,
are trained to the exercise of discrimination; they
are also taught most invaluable economic truths;
for as they are made acquainted with the details
of business, they will soon comprehend the true
nature and functions of capital. It is impossible

to conceive any training which is more fitted to qualify labourers for the successful establishment of such an institution as the Rochdale Cooperative Manufactory.

I cannot leave this subject without referring to a novel and most interesting application of the cooperative principle to the cultivation of land. A Suffolk gentleman, Mr Gurdon of Assington Hall, was greatly struck with the deplorable poverty of the labourers, employed on his own, and neighbouring estates. He long endeavoured to discover some efficient remedy; and about thirty years since he commenced a scheme, the success of which promises vast good to our labouring population. Mr Gurdon resolved to make the labourers his tenants; he let the land to them, charging them the ordinary rent which would be paid by a tenant-farmer. He advanced them sufficient capital to cultivate the land, and this capital was to be re-paid in a certain number of years. Mr Gurdon has now been repaid all the capital which he originally advanced, and these farms are in the highest state of cultivation. The labourers, as at Rochdale, select from amongst their own body a committee of management, and those who are employed, receive the ordinary agricultural wages. The profits are divided according to a plan very similar to that which has been adopted at Rochdale. The

labourers who cultivate these farms, have been socially, materially, and morally so much improved,
that it can be scarcely believed that they were
once in the same miserable condition as the ordinary agricultural labourers in the surrounding district.

It seems to me that there is only one danger
which can imperil the continued success of this
scheme. The labourers who cultivate these farms
are tenants, and they therefore possess no security
of tenure. Mr Gurdon is far too benevolent ever
to disturb them, but it is possible that his succes-
sor might be anxious to appropriate to himself all
the additional value which has been given to the
land, by the careful cultivation of these labouring
tenants. This possible danger ought perhaps not to
be regretted ; for it may induce the scheme to assume a higher developement. It must be admitted
that by this experiment it has been conclusively
proved, that associations of labourers can successfully cultivate land, even when they rent it. How
much greater then would be the success achieved, if
such associations owned, instead of rented the land
which they cultivate. There would then be no
difficulty about insuring fixity of tenure, and the
labourers could never be in the least degree discouraged, by feeling that the improvements which
their careful culture effected in the land might be

at any time appropriated by the individual to whom the land belonged. Such an association would be a true cooperative society; cooperation is for many reasons particularly adapted to agriculture; this branch of industry offers few temptations for speculation, and its profits are not subject to great fluctuations; the cotton-trade on the other hand has always been characterised by recurring periods of great prosperity, and of corresponding adversity.

All these various industrial schemes may be regarded as affording evidence, that the present economic relations between employers and employed have been proved to be unsatisfactory, and are therefore destined to be modified. It would be idle to attempt either to describe the exact form which this modification will assume, or to predict the rapidity with which the change may be wrought. I have merely striven to show you the benefits which result from new economic arrangments which have already been partially adopted. If we desire to hasten the change, we can only do so by bringing into operation whatever agencies may tend to give the labourer those qualities which the new state of things requires. I have already expressed an opinion that the labourer's defects chiefly arise from a want of education. But it may perhaps be said, What can be

done to promote education? Books are cheap,
teachers are abundant, and schools are numerous
and good. If however all this is admitted, it only
seems to bring the following question more forcibly
home to us. Ought the government to extend to
the whole labouring population those compulsory
provisions, which have secured the education of the
factory children? No child, under nine years of
age, is permitted to be employed in a cotton or
woollen manufactory, and a child between nine
and thirteen years of age is only allowed to work
so many hours a week, and the employer of the
child can at any time under a severe penalty, be
called upon to produce a certificate, that the child
has attended school so many hours in each week;
the school moreover must be one, which the in-
spector has declared to be in a satisfactory state.
The employers were at first bitterly opposed to
this legislation and vehemently affirmed that
such interference on the part of the State would
utterly destroy their manufacturing industry.
These predictions have been as signally falsified, as
were the predictions of the protectionists, who were
never tired of declaring that the land of this
country could not be cultivated under a free-trade
tariff. Protectionists have long since become free-
traders, and the manufacturers now readily admit
that the Factory Act has effected incalculable advan-

tage. The physical deterioration of the operatives has been arrested. Young children who are kept closely to work for ten or twelve hours a day, have a blight thrown over the freshness of youth, and they grow up with sickly constitutions and with distorted limbs. The daily training of the mind helps the development of the body, and it has been conclusively proved that the children who are at school half the day, and are at work the remaining half, acquire vigour, energy, and intelligence; the efficiency of their labour is thus so much increased, that they really do more work in a day than used to be done by those children who were employed *whole time*, and whose strength and activity were exhausted by such excessive toil.

Similar legislation must be applied to agriculture and to other branches of industry, if it is determined that a large portion of our population shall no longer continue in a state of pitiable ignorance. I have before said that the educational appliances which are liberally provided at the present day do not reach the root of the evil; there are many localities which possess most excellent schools, and yet the children of the surrounding population, and especially the boys, do not possess even the simplest rudiments of knowledge. I know agricultural villages which are supposed to be well cared for, where the ministers of religion are zealous, where the resident gentlemen are charitable, where the schools are well managed and supported, and yet there is scarcely a youth in these villages who can read with sufficient facility to enable him to understand a newspaper. This melancholy state of things is due to one single circumstance. A father who has a large family to maintain on ten or eleven shillings a week, cannot resist the temptation of taking his children from school directly they can earn the smallest pittance. A child of eight or nine years of age receives threepence a day for holloaing at crows, and a ploughboy of about the same age obtains two shillings a week; the father, although he does an irreparable injury to his children, yet perhaps scarcely deserves to be blamed. In the first place, he is himself ignorant, and he therefore cannot estimate the blessings of education; and secondly, two shillings added to his income, increases it by nearly 20 per cent.; he cannot therefore forego this augmentation of his resources without an amount of self-denial, of which we can form no conception. Ignorance will consequently continue from generation to generation, if education is not enforced by some compulsory regulations. The experience of the Factory Acts is most valuable; it shows that education can not only be promoted but secured by proper legislation, and the gratifying result is also demonstrated, that neither parents nor employers suffer any pecuniary loss if the children are made to attend school a certain number of hours per day; their labour becomes so much more efficient, that the employer can afford to pay them the same wages for a smaller number of hours of work. It is however possible that some temporary pecuniary loss may have to be borne; thus the employers may have to pay a somewhat higher price for juvenile labour, because its aggregate supply would be virtually diminished by these restrictions. A parent may also have to endure some temporary sacrifice, if he is not permitted to exercise absolute control over the labour of his children. But any such temporary disadvantage becomes insignificant when it is compared with ulterior consequences. A man who is allowed to grow up with his mind entirely neglected has inflicted upon him a grievous wrong; he is cut off from the surest and noblest sources of happiness, and even if he is regarded simply as an agent for the production of wealth, he is made by ignorance comparatively useless and inefficient. An unintelligent labourer is like a machine which works roughly, because no care was taken about the putting together of its various parts, which, perfect themselves, might have been so combined

that the machine would achieve completeness in
all its operations. Consequently, ignorance, by
impairing the efficiency of labour, inflicts upon the
nation a most serious pecuniary loss. But this
is not all; crime, and that improvidence which
inevitably produces destitution, are in a great
degree caused by ignorance. Our criminal and
our pauper population involve an expenditure
which is an onerous burden upon our industry.
Hence if our labourers were better educated, the
nation would be relieved from some of its most
severe imposts; labour would become more efficient, and thus the production of wealth would be
stimulated; the people would then possess sufficient intelligence to enable them to combine and
to cooperate for a common object; the condition
of the industrial classes would thus be regenerated, and the happiness and glory of the country
would grow, as its poverty and crime diminished.
We ought not to rest contented with our civilization, whilst nearly 130,000 criminals are annually
convicted in England and Wales, and whilst one
out of every twenty of our population is a pauper.
The last fact is perhaps a more melancholy one
than the first. A crime is often the result of some
sudden outburst of passion; but wide-spread
pauperism exhibits a settled evil which is permanently in operation. The existence of this poverty

is in itself a reproach, and its legalized relief is fraught with manifold evil. Many of those who claim parochial support, are, and will always continue to be the indolent, the profligate, and the intemperate; many too have become paupers, either because their parents have neglected them, or because they have been stricken down by diseases which have been chiefly generated by insufficient food, and by the pestilential air of unwholesome dwellings. These causes which produce poverty will gradually cease to operate, as the labourers become sufficiently advanced to raise their condition by cooperative efforts; then they will not be dependent on others to relieve them either in old age or in sickness. Now, when a man's strength is exhausted, either by old age or sickness, it seems to be considered that his proper destiny is to live upon the parish rates. Until that day comes, when a life of toil shall lead to some happier result than this, every Englishman should feel that a heavy stigma rests upon his country. This is one reason why I so earnestly desire some change in our existing economic relations; as long as the labourer simply works for hire, I know his condition will not be materially improved; I also know, that if the efficiency of labour is to be maintained, and if England is to continue to grow in wealth, happiness, and prosperity, the labourers must participate in the profits yielded by their industry. The object I have had in view in this Chapter has been to show you, how Cooperation in its various forms will enable this participation in profits to be accomplished.

CHAPTER IV.

The Causes which regulate Wages.

IT is essential to our investigations, that a clear conception should be obtained of the causes which regulate the wages which are paid in any employment. It is not unfrequently assumed, that wages are only controlled by the arbitrary caprice of the employer. If therefore they are supposed to be too low, he alone is blamed; and he is often denounced, as if greed and selfishness prompted him to deprive the labourer of his just reward. Such opinions as these are often maintained by well intentioned men, and consequently their philanthropy becomes a futile and misdirected effort. These opinions are also the origin of much of that ill-feeling which exists between employers and employed; for accusations will constantly be made against employers, if labourers believe that the amount of wages they receive is solely determined by the will of those for whom they work. It is therefore most important to show that wages are regulated by fixed and well ascertained laws; and that these laws are as certain in their operation, as those which control physical nature. If a body is in motion, and you wish to change its direction and velocity, you can only do so by acting on some of the causes which produce this motion. In the same way, if you wish to alter the wages paid to any class of labourers, you can only do so by first ascertaining, and then acting upon some of the causes which determine the particular rate of wages which may happen to be paid. I will therefore proceed to consider the various circumstances which regulate the remuneration of labour.

I think that you are all sufficiently acquainted with the elementary principles of Political Economy, to know that the circulating capital of a country is its wage-fund. Hence if we desire to calculate the average money wages received by each labourer, we have simply to divide the amount of this capital by the number of the labouring population. It is therefore evident that the average money wages cannot be increased, unless either the circulating capital is augmented, or the number of the labouring population is diminished. I have used the expression 'money wages,' because the price of commodities is one element, in determining the actual remuneration which the labourer receives; for it is manifest, that if the articles which he is accustomed to purchase advance 20 per cent. in price, his real wages would be diminished, although his wages, estimated in money, might have increased 10 per cent. In order to avoid complexity of language, I shall assume, that there is no change in the prices of commodities, and hence the word wages will signify both the real and the pecuniary remuneration of the labourer. Since therefore it has been shown that the average rate of wages is regulated by a ratio between capital and population; we are naturally led to consider the causes which effect the increase and decrease both of capital and population.

In a wealthy country such as England, far more capital is accumulated than her own industry requires. There is scarcely a government to whom we have not lent money, and scarcely any great public work, in any quarter of the world, for which English capital is not freely subscribed. By our aid, railways will be carried within sight of the perpetual snows of the Himalayas; our steamers will traverse the remote regions of central Asia, and even young countries commencing a career of progress seek the aid of England's capital; for instance, it has been shown that England supplied £13,500,000 for the Grand Trunk Railway of Canada; whereas Canada, and the United States together, scarcely subscribed £500,000. From these remarks, it is evident that only a portion, and perhaps not a large portion of the wealth which is annually saved in this country, is invested in our own industry. If wages therefore are at any time very low, this cannot be due to an insufficient supply of capital, because the wage-fund could be immediately greatly increased if we limited the amount of capital which we annually embark in foreign investments. In this respect, less wealthy countries offer a striking contrast when compared with England. Thus the capital hitherto possessed by India has been most inadequate for the development of her vast natural resources; and labour in India has consequently been worse remunerated than probably in any other country. The ryot could do little more than supply himself with the barest necessaries of life. The importation of capital into India would therefore necessarily augment the wage-fund, and would increase the remuneration of labour. Capital has been constantly flowing into India from England during the last few years. Since 1853, we have subscribed not less than £40,000,000 for Indian Railways. A considerable portion of this sum has been paid to native labourers, and the result has been, that wages in the districts which are traversed by these railways, have certainly within a short time, advanced not less than

100 per cent. But if foreign countries should send capital to England, it would produce no perceptible effect upon the current rate of wages in this country. The capital thus sent would probably be invested in our leading securities; their price would rise, and English holders would thus be induced to sell out, and would probably invest their money in some foreign undertaking. We must have all observed, that directly the rate of interest declines in this country, or, in other words, the supply of capital becomes abundant, it seems that the signal is at once given for the introduction of a foreign loan, or some other undertaking, which will soon cause the surplus capital to be absorbed. It is therefore evident, that the aggregate wealth which is annually saved in England is divided into two portions; one portion is employed as capital to maintain our industry, and the other portion is exported to foreign countries. This conclusion will naturally lead us to inquire, whether it is possible to ascertain the causes which determine the relative magnitude of these two portions, into which the wealth which we annually save is divided.

Experience has abundantly proved, that variations in the amount of capital accumulated, depend upon the profit which can be realised upon this capital, or, in other words, upon the rate of interest. If the general rate of interest should rise, a greater inducement would be offered, to abstain from any expenditure which is not absolutely necessary, and hence more wealth would be annually saved. Since therefore a connection exists between the amount of capital accumulated, and the profit which can be obtained upon this capital, it consequently follows, that the amount of capital invested in any industry is primarily determined, by the average rate of profit which this industry returns. Suppose, for instance, that the woollen trade becomes suddenly prosperous, as it has done during the last four years; every woollen manufacturer will be anxious to extend his business as much as possible. Capital, which before he might have invested in some foreign speculations, he will now employ in his own business, and he will use his credit to borrow capital from others, who will be induced to lend it him, in consequence of the high rate of interest which he can now afford to pay them. If therefore the profits in any branch of industry increase, the capital employed in it might soon be doubled; capital will in a similar way be withdrawn, if trade is depressed by adverse circumstances. During the continuance of the American Civil War, the manufacture of cotton yielded no profit. Immense sums of capital previously employed in this industry, have consequently been sent to the London Money Market to be invested in various securities, both home and foreign. This caused the supply of capital to be so abundant, that an unprecedently large number of new loans and various joint-stock companies were started.

The two examples to which allusion has just been made, clearly show that as the profits of any trade decrease or increase, the capital employed in it will be either immediately diminished or augmented. But although there is thus a supply of capital always ready to satisfy any demand, yet additional labour, if it is required in any trade, cannot be provided with the same facility. The various processes which are carried on in any industry need a particular skill, which cannot be acquired without previous training and practice. No one can visit a cotton manufactory, without observing how marvellously delicate are some of the manipulations which human hands perform, as the raw material is gradually spun and woven into cotton cloth. In other branches of industry, human dexterity shows equally astonishing results. I have often stood and watched with almost bewildered amazement, the glass-blowing which can be daily seen at Birmingham. A man places a blow-pipe in a cauldron of molten glass. He seems instinctively to dip up the precise quantity of glass he requires. His object, we will suppose, is to make a wine-decanter, similar in every respect to one

which has been made before.   He begins blowing,
twirling and twisting, and in a few moments the
decanter is made, and the nicest eye fails to discover the slightest difference in size or shape, between it and the one which has served as a model.
Yet whilst he was doing his work, apparently with
careless ease; his eye, his hand, and the power of
his breath, must have adjusted and controlled various forces, which are far too complicated in their
operation to be traced by the most refined mathematical analysis.   But this skill of the Lancashire
cotton operative, or the Birmingham glass-blower,
is special; and if either was to change his employment for that of the other, it would be long before
he was little better than a useless bungler.

The impossibility of immediately augmenting
to a great extent the labour adapted to carry on
a particular branch of industry, produces some very
important results, which may be best illustrated by
an example.   Let us suppose, and it is really what
has actually occurred during the last four years,
that the woollen trade has suddenly been made extremely active, by a large increase in both the home
and foreign demand for woollen goods; prices rise,
and perhaps it is not too much to assume, that
the profits of the manufacturers are soon doubled.
Every one consequently endeavours to extend his
business as much as possible; labour is eagerly

competed for, and wages greatly increase. But this rise in wages would not take place if the additional labour which is required, could be obtained from other employments; since a manufacturer would naturally say: if I require additional labour, I would rather give fifty per cent. more to one who has been accustomed to the industry, than employ a bungler who has never been in a woollen mill before, for such a labourer will probably injure the machinery, and be a hindrance to others. It therefore follows, that within certain limits, the wages which any class of labourers receive, depend upon the average rate of profit which may happen to be realised in the trade in which they are engaged; because, if profits increase, more capital will be invested in this particular branch of industry, and consequently the wage-fund will be augmented.

In stating this proposition, I have been careful to employ the qualifying phrase '*within certain limits*,' since it can be readily proved that unless artificial restrictions are imposed, there is a certain rate of wages which may be said naturally to belong to each employment, and towards this natural rate, wages are constantly tending to approximate. Thus although a sudden improvement in the woollen trade may cause wages to advance fifty per cent., yet this rise cannot be permanently maintained; for if this particular kind of labour receives such exceptionally high remuneration, more and more labour would be gradually attracted to the trade, and a greater number of children would be trained to follow it. The supply of labour would thus be steadily augmented, and wages would consequently gradually decline.

It is not however difficult to show, that in some branches of industry, labour must permanently receive a higher remuneration than in others. Some trades, for instance, require great skill on behalf of the workmen. This skill can perhaps only be attained after a long and expensive training, and perhaps training will not be sufficient, unless a person is as it were specially endowed by nature; thus those workmen who can grind a lens, or construct a chronometer, with the mathematical accuracy which is now demanded, are so few in number, that their peculiar skill may be regarded as a monopoly, which they can dispose of at an extremely high price; the wages which they receive are not affected by the competition of the general body of labourers, but are chiefly determined by the price which people are willing to give, for such delicate and perfect instruments. Again, proficiency in many kinds of industry can only be acquired after long practice; the young beginner in fact needs a teacher, who must be remunerated. Thus in the

engineering trade, a youth has to pass an apprenticeship of seven years; during this time he receives scarcely any wages. During the last three
years of his apprenticeship, his labour may become useful, and the employer is thus remunerated
for the trouble and expense of instructing him.
A parent would not of course make the sacrifice
which is required, if he thus apprentices his son
for seven years, unless he supposed that his son
would be abundantly compensated by receiving in
after life higher wages, than if he had been brought
up to some less skilled industry which needed no
apprenticeship. Some occupations are also much
more dangerous and unhealthy than others. Thus
miners incur many risks, and the average period
of their life is shortened by many years, in consequence of the bad air which they are generally
obliged to breathe. A miner must consequently
receive higher wages than agricultural labourers,
in order to compensate him for these disadvantages which are connected with his employment.
Some kinds of labour cannot be carried on if the
weather is unfavourable. Thus building is often
to a great extent stopped during the winter
months. The wages which are earned by masons
and bricklayers, must therefore be sufficient to
remunerate them for the time during which they
are kept out of work. It therefore appears that

the average remuneration which labour receives in different employments is regulated by various circumstances, such as skill, the regularity or irregularity of the employment, and the healthiness or unhealthiness of the occupation. Hence a certain rate of wages which may be termed a natural rate, belongs to each kind of labour; although it may be impossible to deduce from *à priori* reasoning, what may be the exact amount of this natural rate in any particular case. Thus suppose agricultural labourers earn ten shillings a week, we cannot say beforehand whether miners in the same district will earn fourteen or eighteen shillings a week. We may however be quite certain that their wages will be higher than those of the agricultural labourers; and the additional amount which they receive may be regarded as an adequate compensation, for the various disadvantages which are connected with mining, when compared with agriculture.

Now that we have established the proposition, that in different employments, different rates of wages must necessarily prevail, let us next proceed to prove, that the wages paid in any industry are not the result either of caprice or chance, but are regulated by principles, which are as certain in their operation, as are the physical forces from which all natural phenomena result. In order

to illustrate this truth, let it be supposed that the
wages of the agricultural labourer are ten shillings
a week, and that no artificial impediments prevent
him from offering his labour wherever it will be
best remunerated. It may with justice be affirmed,
that every able-bodied man in our country, ought
to be able to obtain more than ten shillings a week
for his labour; such an amount will not provide
him and his family a sufficiency of the necessaries of life. It is impossible for him to make
any adequate provision for old age or sickness,
and hence he and those who are dependent on
him, are constantly verging on a state of pauperism.
The result is, that no insignificant portion of our
population are paupers; a fact which is a serious
disgrace to a country so wealthy as our own. A
man who only earns ten shillings a week is so poor,
that he is almost compelled to make his children
labour directly they can obtain even the smallest
wages. His children are constantly sent to work
when they are only eight or nine years old; they
have not acquired even the first rudiments of
education, and it is consequently no exaggeration
to say, that our agricultural population as a general
rule can neither read nor write. Improved schools
and large educational grants entirely fail to attack
the real source of this evil, and it is a truism to
say that ignorance is one of the chief causes of

intemperance and vice. But pauperism, intemperance, and vice, are not only a disgrace to the nation, but entail upon it a heavy pecuniary burden. The whole community may therefore be considered to suffer if any class of labourers are unable to earn sufficient wages. When therefore we contemplate the miserable condition of the agricultural labourers, this question is naturally suggested, Is there any one who at the present time can be fairly blamed for the existence of this poverty? Are their employers hard-hearted and unjust? And since it has been shown that the State is interested that no class of labourers should be underpaid, ought the law to interfere and decree, that no able-bodied man should receive less than fifteen shillings a week? I shall endeavour to prove to you, that such State interference would not only be futile, but would be also highly pernicious, and I shall also seek to prove, that the employers who pay these small wages cannot be fairly blamed.

It follows from our previous remarks, that the amount of capital employed in agriculture, and therefore the aggregate amount of wages distributed amongst the agricultural labourers, depends upon the profits which farming yields. A person when he takes a farm, calculates as nearly as possible what his profits will be, after he has paid his rent, the wages of his labourers, and all other expenses. He will not of course take the farm, if he does not think he will obtain a proper rate of interest for his capital, and for his labour of superintendence. We will assume that the farm he intends to take is one of 800 acres, and that he requires a capital of £6000 for the proper cultivation of this farm; he pays his able-bodied labourers ten shillings a week, and the aggregate amount he spends in wages during the year is £800. His profits are £600, or, in other words, 10 per cent. on his capital. We believe that these assumed figures represent with considerable accuracy a real case. Now it cannot be said that 10 per cent. is too large a trade profit, and therefore the farmer by no means realizes large gains, although his labourers are underpaid. Let it now be supposed that the law interferes, and decrees that no able-bodied labourer shall receive less than fifteen shillings a week. The farmer would, if he employed the same number of labourers, now pay £1200 a year, instead of £800 a year in wages, and his profit would be reduced from £600 to £200. This would only represent an interest of $3\frac{1}{2}$ per cent. on his capital, and he of course would not under these circumstances continue such an unremunerative occupation, since he could obtain a larger interest on his capital without any trouble or risk, if he invested his money in some ordinary security, such as bank or railway shares. The absurdity of legislating to control wages is thus clearly demonstrated.

It may however perhaps be argued, that if the farmers were compelled by law to raise their wages, they might be compensated, either by a rise in the price of their produce, or by a reduction in their rents. Let us in the first place consider, whether a rise in the price of produce thus artificially created, would really attain the objects sought. It is not difficult to show, that it would be impossible to maintain an artificial rise in the price of any produce. The price of a commodity is regulated by demand and supply, and the demand, as well as the supply, are influenced, not by the market of one country, but by the market of the whole world. Thus, if manufacturers were compelled to increase the price of their goods by 10 per cent., in order to compensate themselves for the higher wages which the law or any other power decree that they should pay; the demand for these goods would be most seriously diminished; a successful competition could probably be no longer carried on with other countries either in the home or foreign markets; their trade might in this way be almost ruined; their operations would at any rate be greatly restricted; they would consequently employ much less labour, and although they might pay higher wages, the aggregate amount which they would distribute in wages would be greatly diminished. Consequently the labourers would be injured instead of benefited, if an increase in the price of commodities, was the result of artificial arrangements to raise the rate of wages.

It would be equally futile, to attempt to raise the wages of agricultural labourers by a compulsory reduction in the rent of land. There is always a great deal of land which is so poor, that it only just pays the expense of cultivation. This land therefore would be thrown out of cultivation, if the cost of tilling it was greatly augmented by an enforced rise in wages. A considerable area of land would also be laid down in pasture, if the cost of labour was considerably enhanced. Hence less labour would be employed in agriculture, and the aggregate amount distributed in wages amongst agricultural labourers would be diminished. It therefore appears, that the consequences would ultimately be equally disastrous to the labourers, whether rents were reduced or the price of produce increased, as the result of an augmentation of wages produced by compulsory measures. Consequently any attempt to regulate wages by compulsory enactments would either be futile or would be highly injurious to those who were intended to be

benefited. All therefore that the legislature can
do, is to watch with scrupulous care, that nothing
prevents wages being freely controlled by demand
and supply. It should be considered that the
working man has a commodity, namely, his labour,
to dispose of, and it is most desirable that he
should have the fullest opportunity of disposing
of his labour, on the best possible terms. We
shall presently inquire whether or not some of
the conditions connected with our poor law system operate in such a manner, that many at least
of our labourers are virtually restricted to a district, and cannot therefore obtain so high a price
for their labour, as if they were freely permitted to
offer it in the open market.

If it was more clearly understood, that the
price of labour was regulated in the same way
as the price of any commodity such as wheat,
by demand and supply, professed philanthropists
would cease to talk idle nonsense about hard-
hearted employers, and the labourers themselves
would at once see what is the origin of their
poverty, and what are the means which would be
effectual in improving their condition. If a commodity declines in price, it must be because the
demand for it is diminished, or its supply is increased. If it is desired to advance its price, the
demand must be augmented, or the supply dimi-

nished. In the same way, if it is desired to raise the rate of wages, either more capital must be invested in industry, or the number of the labouring population must be diminished. If the capital invested in industry increases more rapidly than the number of the labouring population, wages must advance. The progress of England during the last few years, has been marked by a great increase both in wealth and population. It can however be conclusively proved that capital has increased more than population, and wages consequently have advanced. This advance in wages has been greater in some employments than in others. The vast extension of our foreign trade and commerce, has caused a great demand for manufacturing and building operatives, artizans, shipwrights, &c.; and their wages have consequently advanced in a much greater ratio than the wages of agricultural labourers. It becomes very important to consider, whether labour is likely to continue to obtain a larger remuneration; and we will therefore proceed to investigate various circumstances which bear upon this question.

It is evident from the remarks I have already made, that the amount of capital invested in industry, is mainly regulated by the amount of profit which can be realized. We must therefore endeavour to ascertain, what are the circumstances

which are likely to affect the future rate of trade
profit. It will also be necessary to consider some
of the various circumstances, which may cause
either an increase or a decrease in our population.
On the one hand, marriages amongst our labouring
population have hitherto varied with their prosperity; but, on the other hand, it is possible that if
their condition was improved, they would become
more prudent with regard to marriage. An immense number of the working classes during the
last few years have emigrated. We must consequently inquire, whether it is probable that this
emigration will continue, on a larger or smaller
scale. The poverty of our poor has in various ways
exerted a most powerful check upon population.
The poorer children of this country have been almost decimated by diseases engendered, not only
by want of food, but also by the air which they
are compelled to breathe, in dwellings which are
not fit for human beings to live in. These and
various other circumstances must be discussed, if
we seek to form an estimate of the probable increase in our population, compared with the probable future accumulation of capital.

When considering the remuneration which labour is destined to receive, the essential distinction between real and money wages must be very
carefully borne in mind. It is evident that if the

commodities which the labourer ordinarily purchases advance in price 20 per cent., his real wages
would be seriously diminished, although nominally
they might be advanced 5 or 10 per cent. It
therefore appears that the price of food, and also
the price of the various other commodities which
the labourer purchases, has a very essential bearing upon our investigations. Let it for instance
be assumed, that the manufacturing operative earns
forty shillings a week, and that owing to an advance
in prices, this forty shillings will only exchange for
the same quantity of commodities as could formerly be purchased for thirty-five shillings. In
order therefore that the labourer might not be
worse off, his wages ought to be advanced from
thirty-five to forty shillings a-week. But who is to
pay these extra wages ? If the manufacturer pays
them, his profits will decrease, and he will be induced to diminish the amount of capital invested
in his business; whereas it would be necessary to
increase the amount of capital, because if those
whom he may employ are to receive higher wages,
the wage-fund must be augmented. Again, if the
manufacturers advance the price of their goods
in order to pay their labourers higher wages, their
trade would manifestly suffer, because the demand
for a commodity depends upon its price. But if
the trade suffered, the labourers must be injured,

since manufacturers would contract their operations and employ fewer hands. It therefore follows that a rise in the price of the commodities
which the labourers purchase, must inflict a real
loss upon them, because this rise in price does not
produce any advantage to the employer, which
would enable him to compensate his labourers
for the greater expense which their living now
entails.

I will however bring forward some further considerations, in order to show you, that of all the
causes which promote the prosperity of the labourer, none are more efficient than cheap food
and cheap clothing. I have frequently remarked,
that the amount of capital which is invested in
our industry, depends upon the amount of profit
which can be realised. This proposition is moreover of special applicability, with regard to such
a country as England; each year the capital which
we accumulate is more freely embarked in foreign
investments. The aggregate savings of the country are therefore divided into two portions, which
are diverted into distinct channels. One of these
portions represents the capital which we send to
other countries, the other portion represents the
capital which we invest in our own industry. The
relative magnitude of these two portions will evidently be determined by the returns which are

yielded upon capital when invested abroad, compared with the returns which are yielded when
it is invested at home. If, for instance, the rate
of profit increased in India, and declined in England, a greater portion of our national capital
would be sent to India, and a smaller portion
would be retained, to be invested in our own industry. Hence the rate of profit which prevails
in England, not only influences the amount of
capital which is saved, but also determines what
portion of this capital shall be retained in this
country. It therefore at once becomes evident,
that the employed are as much interested as are
the employers, in the maintenance of the rate of
profit, because it has been conclusively proved,
that if the rate of profit is diminished, there will
not only be less capital accumulated, but an increasing portion of that which is accumulated will
be exported to foreign countries. Let us therefore seek to discover some of the circumstances
which exert the most powerful effect in sustaining
the rate of profit.

It is scarcely necessary to remark, that any
circumstance which increases the efficiency of labour will tend to augment the rate of profit; for
if labour is made more efficient, more wealth will
be produced; hence there will be more to distribute both amongst the employers and employed,

and consequently wages and profits may both be augmented. But if on the other hand, those commodities which the labourers chiefly purchase become more expensive, one of two things must occur. In the first place, if his wages are not advanced, the real remuneration of his labour will be diminished; all the articles which he is accustomed to purchase will have advanced in price, and he will have no more money to expend than he had formerly. Secondly, his employers may seek to compensate him by advancing his wages. But even if this were done, a heavy loss would ultimately fall upon the labourer, because it has been proved, that the employed are as much interested in the maintenance of the rate of profit as are the employers. The rate of profit will evidently decline, if it becomes necessary to increase wages, in order to compensate the labourers for an augmentation in the cost of the necessaries of life. It therefore appears that a supply of cheap food obtained either by foreign importation, or by agricultural improvements, is of vital importance to our country. Dear food would perhaps more than any other circumstance imperil our national prosperity; for if the cost of living became relatively greater in this country than in others, one of two things, each of which would be equally disastrous, would occur. In the first place, if wages were not advanced, the condition of our labourers would deteriorate; they would thus be induced to emigrate, and we might be gradually deprived of that supply of skilled and specially trained labour, without which our wealth could not be produced. In the second place, as I have already remarked, the rate of profit in this country would decline, if wages were advanced sufficiently to compensate the labourers for the increase in the cost of living; but if the rate of profit diminished, a greater portion of our capital would be drawn from our own industry, and would be embarked in foreign investments.

As we have shown that the price of food, and of the other ordinary necessaries of life is one important element in determining the real remuneration which labour obtains, it will be interesting to make a few remarks upon the future probable price of those commodities, in the purchase of which working men chiefly spend their wages. It must however be carefully borne in mind, that if we speak of food becoming dearer, we refer to an increased cost of production, and not to a change in the value of money. Thus many competent authorities have affirmed, that the recent gold discoveries in Australia and California, have already caused a marked depreciation in the value of this metal. This depreciation has been variously

estimated at between ten and thirty per cent. Let
us assume it to be twenty per cent.; five sovereigns
will now be worth no more than four sovereigns
were worth, before the discoveries were made. The
money value or price of every commodity will
have advanced in a corresponding ratio. There
is however no reason to suppose that the labourer
would be affected by such a change in the value
of money, because his wages, representing the price
of labour, would increase in the same proportion
as the price of commodities.

These considerations however make it difficult
to decide to what extent the real wages of labour
have advanced during the last few years. As it
has been already stated, it is easy to show by statistics, that in almost all employments there has been
a considerable increase in money wages. But if
those who maintain, that gold has been depreciated
twenty per cent. are correct, it is evident that a
considerable rise in money wages would not necessarily indicate any increase in the real remuneration of labour. The gold question is far too
intricate and complicated to be discussed here;
but after a careful investigation, I certainly incline
to the conclusion, that there has been a depreciation
in the value of gold, although it is almost impossible to estimate its exact amount. The reason
of this difficulty can be very easily explained.

Directly it is attempted to compare the present prices of commodities with their prices previous to the gold discoveries, it is found that there has not been a uniform change in price. Some commodities have increased in price much more than others, whereas the price of others has decreased. This is due to the fact that circumstances have occurred, independently of any change in the value of gold, which have tended to lessen the cost of producing some commodities, and to increase the cost of producing others. Thus, to take an example; our commerce was released from its protective fetters just at the time when the gold deposits in Australia first became known. The market of the world became thrown open to us; immense quantities of wheat were imported, and this importation has of course exerted an influence to reduce the price of corn. But then this question still remains unanswered, Would the price of wheat have been still lower than it is at the present time, if there had been no change in the value of gold? Again there has been a marked rise in the price of meat; this no doubt has been partly caused by an increased demand for meat; and this demand, in consequence of the great expense of bringing live stock from a distance, cannot be supplied by foreign importation. If therefore we wish to form a correct estimate of any change which may have

10

taken place in the real remuneration of labour, our only course is by a detailed examination, to ascertain whether the wages now received will obtain a greater quantity of those commodities which the labourer is accustomed to purchase.

Apart from any change in the value of the precious metals, which would alike affect the price of all commodities, it must be remembered that we have proved that the labourer must *pro tanto* suffer, if there is an increase in the cost of producing the commodities which he consumes. We have just alluded to certain circumstances which have exerted an influence upon the cost of two of the principal articles which he consumes, namely, meat and bread. We have shown that bread has been cheapened by the large importation of wheat which has resulted from free trade; this importation may be greatly augmented, since improvements in the means of communication are gradually developing the vast natural resources of many hitherto almost inaccessible regions. For instance, Lord Dalhousie stated in a minute which gave a graphic account of the remarkable deeds achieved during the period of his Indian administration, that if railways and good roads were constructed, and if the navigation of the rivers was improved, the Punjab would be able to supply England with wheat at less than twenty shillings a sack. The valley of the Mississippi could grow sufficient wheat for the whole world. It is even found to be remunerative to send wheat from California, if it realizes twenty-five shillings a sack in the London market. It may therefore fairly be concluded, that on the average of years, the cost of wheat will not increase, although as our population advances, the demand for wheat will steadily augment. No proposition of more fundamental importance than this can be established, with regard to the future position of the British labourer. Political Economists have again and again proved, that corn and all agricultural produce will gradually become more expensive as our population increases, and that therefore the condition of the labourer gradually deteriorates as population advances. This no doubt would be true, if we were restricted to our own soil for obtaining our supplies of food, because with a larger population, there would be a greater demand for agricultural produce. This additional demand would have to be satisfied, by bringing inferior soils into cultivation, and produce would consequently be raised from it at a greater cost. This prospective augmentation of the cost of food in an advancing country, has thrown a gloom over the speculations of those Political Economists, who apparently failed to foresee the great results of Free Trade. It may now without exaggeration be said, that nothing will exert a more powerful influence in maintaining the progressive prosperity of this country, than an importation of cheap corn, for it is thus that our population will be able to increase, without any deterioration in the condition of the labourer.

The tendency which agricultural produce has to increase in cost as population advances, is corroborated by a decided rise in the price of meat. Live stock, as we have before said, cannot without great difficulty be imported from a distance. Our own soil must therefore produce nearly all the fresh meat which we require; it may consequently be regarded as almost certain that fresh meat will continue to advance in price, although much more live stock will probably be kept on our own soil, when the English farmer who is always slow to perceive a change, is fully impressed with the fact, that wheat is likely to be always very cheap, and meat comparatively dear. When this fact is recognised, our system of agriculture will be changed ; less wheat will be grown, and a greater quantity of beef and mutton will be produced.

From these considerations we may perhaps fairly conclude, that cheap corn will compensate the labourer for the increased dearness of meat. The improvements which have been effected in manufacturing industry, since the general introduction of steam, have considerably diminished the cost of most articles of wearing apparel. Machinery is now so perfect, that we can hardly anticipate that the processes of manufacturing are likely to be considerably cheapened. There will therefore be no counteracting influence to prevent a rise in the value of manufactured goods, if raw material should become more expensive, and if the manufacturing operative should be better paid. With regard to one great branch of our industry, there seems to be every prospect that the raw material will not, at any rate for a long time to come, be so cheap as it was a few years since. Slavery has now been happily abolished in the United States. The cultivation of cotton which was carried on almost entirely by slave-labour, has received a rude shock, and many years must elapse before this industry can be restored to its former prosperity. I have however little doubt that ultimately this industry, supported as it will be by free labour, will obtain a greater prosperity than it has ever enjoyed before; the labour of the slave must be comparatively unproductive, for when a human being is degraded to the condition of a brute, he cannot possess skill, energy, prudence, or any other industrial virtue. It may however be reasonably expected, that a considerable time will be required to consummate this economic transition from slave to free labour, and during this transitional period, raw cotton will probably be dearer than it has been in past years. There are other reasons which strengthen the opinion that cotton goods are likely to be permanently dearer than they have been. Many of the operatives who have been lately thrown out of work, have been drafted into other employments, and have settled in new localities. Many thousands have also emigrated; the cotton trade has therefore to a great extent lost its skilled and trained labour, and this will tend to increase the cost of manufacture.

With regard to other branches of manufacturing industry, there has lately been an extraordinary advance in the value of the raw material. It is of course natural that this should have occurred; the demand for wool and flax must be greatly augmented, as the supply of raw cotton becomes diminished. Other circumstances moreover will tend to increase the value of wool and flax; for considering our own country alone, the demand for woollen and linen cloth has during the last few years been greatly augmented. Between 1847 and the present time, our export trade has been nearly trebled, and in no department of industry has this growth of our foreign trade been more strikingly exhibited, than in the export of manufactured goods. I therefore think that the balance of evidence will certainly support the opinion, that

woollen, cotton, and linen cloths, are likely to become dearer.

Next to food and wearing apparel, the chief
item in a working man's expenditure is his house
rent. Now there can be no doubt that house rent
has greatly increased during the last few years.
As population advances, the demand for houses
becomes greater; as towns extend, land becomes
more valuable, and the space which was formerly
occupied by labourers' dwellings, is gradually en-
croached upon by warehouses, shops, streets, &c.
So much has this been the case in our large towns,
that there is now a positive dearth of houses suitable to labourers; as a consequence, house rent has
not only greatly advanced, but a worse evil than
this has arisen, for labourers are huddled and
packed together in a manner which destroys health,
and which ignores the decencies of life. This evil
is at the present time so glaring in London, that it
has aroused the attention of the legislature; a provision has therefore been wisely enacted, that all
new railways which enter the metropolis, shall be
compelled to issue weekly tickets for a shilling, so
that labourers who are employed in London, may
be able to live at a considerable distance from the
metropolis. I anticipate important results from
this legislation; for it seems to remove one of the
greatest difficulties which the working man has to

contend with; since at the present time, it is almost impossible for him to obtain a healthy and a comfortable house, at such a price as he can afford to pay.

I have now considered some of the chief circumstances which affect, or are likely to affect, the cost of living, so far as the working man is concerned. On such a subject I know it would be rash to make positive predictions, but I cannot help inclining to the opinion, that the labourer ought to expect, that the cost of living in this country is more likely to increase than to decrease. I state this conclusion independently of any change in the value of money; such a change need necessarily only affect those who have fixed money payments, either to make or to receive. If gold becomes depreciated, the price of labour would rise proportionately to the rise in the prices of all commodities; and this rise in money wages need not diminish the profits of the employer, because the money value of these profits would also advance proportionately to the general rise in prices. But much more serious consequences will ensue, if the commodities which the labourer consumes become more expensive to produce, and thus increase his cost of living. If this should occur, he cannot hope to be compensated for the loss which he would then suffer; for we have shown that if his wages were advanced, his master's profits would be diminished. This diminution of profits would cause less capital to be invested in industry, and therefore in the end, a less aggregate amount would be distributed in wages.

The labourer may receive an adequate compensation for the loss which he will suffer from an increase in the cost of living, if his labour can be made more productive; for then higher wages might be paid to him, without encroaching upon the employers' profits. Let us therefore inquire, what is the prospect that industry may be rendered more efficient. I have already dwelt somewhat emphatically upon the many evils which result from the labourer having no share in the profits which are realised by his industry. I have endeavoured to show, that whilst he remains in this position, it cannot be reasonably supposed that he will work with great energy, intelligence, or care. Employers naturally complain that their labourers feel no concern about their masters' interest. I again repeat that this must always continue to be the case, whilst employers and employed are not united by any of the feelings which arise from common pecuniary interest. Every employer who has thought upon this subject will bear me out in the opinion, that it is difficult to exaggerate the loss which he suffers from his labourers' being in many

respects so inefficient. I have constantly heard
employers say, that they would willingly pay a
large annual sum, if they could feel sure that the
labourers would do everything in their power to
promote their masters' interest. This being the
case, it seems to me somewhat singular that employers do not endeavour to create some common
pecuniary interest between themselves and those
whom they employ; for it is the absence of this
which causes those evils, in regard to which complaints are so often heard. If the owner of a
business feels that its success mainly depends upon
the activity of some one whom he has appointed
to be manager, he knows that the best plan to
stimulate this manager to exert himself to the utmost, is to promise him, in addition to a fixed
salary, a certain share of the aggregate profits
which are realised. This plan has been constantly
adopted in joint-stock companies; for it has been
often proved that the prosperity of a joint-stock
company chiefly depends upon its manager; in fact,
wherever it has been felt to be peculiarly important that any one connected with a business should
put forth all his energies and all his powers, he is
encouraged to do so, by a promise of a share of
the profits realised. The shipowner knows that
upon the captain of a vessel, the success, or failure,
of a voyage depends; he therefore encourages the

zeal or enterprise of the captain, by making him a participator in the profits which may be obtained. Why therefore should not the same principle be extended to others who are engaged in a business? Why should not the labourer, in the same way as the manager, be made more energetic, more intelligent, and more zealous, by sharing the profits which his industry yields? It may of course be argued, that the aggregate profits which the employer obtains would be diminished, if he gave his labourers a certain portion of these profits. We, however, on the contrary, maintain that the industry of the labourer would in every respect be rendered so much more efficient, and therefore so much more productive, that the employer would be far more than compensated for the portion of his profits which he might thus relinquish in favour of his labourers. I am not aware that the sharing of profits between employers and employed, which may be termed copartnership, has ever been attempted in our own country, except in the partial way to which we have already alluded, where a certain share of the profits has been occasionally given to such persons, as the manager of a joint-stock company, or a sea-captain. But in Paris, a copartnership such as we have described, has achieved the most gratifying and most encouraging results. The circumstances under which the experiment was made have been often described; but they are so interesting and so instructive, that I venture briefly to repeat them once more.

M. Leclaire was a house-decorator, who carried on a very large business, and employed 200 men. He, like so many other employers, found that his trade was suffering, and that he was subject to great annoyance, in consequence of the carelessness and apathy of his men. The evil had grown to such an extent, that he had resolved to relinquish his business, if some improvement could not be effected. He felt that some decided remedy was required. He therefore assembled his men, told them that they had hitherto shown no anxiety to promote his interest, and that he was desirous to create some common sympathy between them and himself, by making them, to a certain degree, participate in the profits realised. He therefore promised annually to distribute amongst his workmen, a certain portion of his aggregate profits. M. Leclaire most positively affirms, that he has been, even in a pecuniary sense, abundantly recompensed for the share of the profits which he thus gave to his workmen. An entire change was produced in their conduct and in their demeanour. A certain *esprit de corps* seemed to be created amongst them, which prompted each one to exert himself to the utmost. Their work was now always well done; and it was quite unnecessary to have anyone to overlook them.

I will allude to one other similar instance of copartnership. The Paris and Orleans Railway Company pay their *employées* the ordinary wages; but, in addition, they distribute amongst them a small portion of the aggregate profits realised. The prospect of obtaining this additional reward produces a marked effect upon the conduct of all the servants on this railway. Slight as this pecuniary incentive may be, it seems to attach them to the Company, and they consequently take a lively interest in everything which may tend to promote its prosperity.

I believe that the most beneficial results would follow, if this system of copartnership was more largely introduced into English industry. It has been repeatedly stated that an advance of wages, which diminishes the profits of the employer, cannot be permanently beneficial to the labourer, because when profits are decreased, there is a smaller inducement to invest capital in industry, and the wage-fund will consequently be diminished. But if labour can be rendered more productive, there would then be a greater amount to distribute amongst both the employers and the employed, and the profits of the employer and the real remuneration of the labourer may both increase.

I do not know any circumstance which would more increase the productiveness of British industry, than if the labourer could be cured of those defects, which are no doubt due to the present complete antagonism of interests between the employers and the employed. How can work be efficiently done, when those whose joint and united efforts are essential, do not labour in cordial unison, but are divided into opposing sections, and are kept asunder by many of those petty feelings which are engendered in those who higgle over a hard-fought bargain? The ordinary objection may be urged, for it will probably be said that such copartnership as we have advocated will never succeed in practice. To such an argument, the only reply that we need make is, that the success of M. Leclaire's experiment, favoured by no special circumstances, may be regarded as conclusive; moreover, I can say, with some confidence, that it is impossible to mention any instance where copartnership has been attempted, and has failed to produce the results which we have attributed to it*.

* I have lately received intelligence of some most interesting experiments, based upon the principle of copartnership. I am rejoiced to find that these copartnerships between employers and employed, are being much more rapidly and extensively introduced in our own country, than could have been anticipated from our *a priori* reasoning. The proprietors of some of our largest commercial concerns

We will now proceed to consider what is the effect of many of those expedients for raising

are changing their establishments into joint-stock companies; they retain the largest portion of the shares in their own possession, and the remaining shares are then offered to those who are employed either as managers, foremen or workmen. The Messrs Crossley of Halifax, Yorkshire, are the owners of probably the largest carpet manufactory in the world. They propose to change their vast establishment into a joint-stock company, the capital of which will be £1,650,000. The Messrs Crossley retain in their own possession shares which represent four-fifths of this capital, the remaining shares they offer to the 4,400 workmen whom they employ; every labourer will thus have an opportunity of becoming a partner. In order still further to explain some of the plans of copartnership, which are proposed to be adopted, we will briefly describe a scheme which has been most admirably devised by the Messrs Briggs, who are large coal proprietors at Methley, near Leeds. They propose to dispose of their coal mines to a joint-stock company, the capital of which, £135,000, is raised by 9000 shares of £15 each. The Messrs Briggs will retain two-thirds of the whole number of shares, and the remaining one-third will be first offered to those who are employed at the mines. The workmen will be able to have on the directory some of their own body to represent them. It is further proposed that if the profits should exceed 10 per cent. after setting aside a fair amount to reimburse capital, one-half the remaining surplus profits shall be distributed amongst the labourers, and that each individual share of this bonus should be proportional to the aggregate wages which he has earned. A most satisfactory cooperation between capital and labour will thus be secured. The Messrs Briggs, who may be regarded as men of great experience, affirm that the plan, even as a commercial experiment, is likely to prove eminently successful. They say with great truth, that labourers who own capital, and who participate in the profits realised, will never resort to strikes, and those unfortunate disputes which have recurred with such disastrous frequency in the coal trade will thus be prevented.

wages, which are most favoured by the labourers.
I need hardly mention, that in discussing this part
of the subject, I must chiefly direct your attention
to the consideration of Strikes and Trades Unions.
I feel that I am now approaching questions which
excite angry passions and bitter antipathies; there
is therefore no subject which it is more essential
to treat with strict impartiality; it is moreover,
one of vast importance. A strike always exhibits
a dogged determination, which seems to show that
the combatants feel as if they were engaged in
a struggle for life or death. On the one hand,
employers believe that if they tamely submit to
the dictation which a strike implies, a fatal blow
will have been struck at the prosperity of the
capitalist class; on the other hand, the employed
show an equal steadfastness of faith that strikes
are necessary, in order to secure to them a proper
remuneration for their labour. They embark on

Messrs Briggs also state, that labour in a coal mine can never be
properly superintended; the portion of profits which may be distributed as a bonus amongst the labourers will stimulate their energy,
and their industry will thus become more efficient.

There is one other example which I cannot refrain from men-
tioning. I have lately seen it reported, that the proprietors of the
Daily News have just signalised the conclusion of a prosperous year,
by distributing a portion of the profits realised, amongst those who are
employed on this journal. Experience justifies a confident hope,
that such wise liberality will be abundantly rewarded.

a strike, fully aware of the terrible cost it may entail upon them, but they seem fully prepared to endure the sacrifice and to bear the suffering, in order to maintain a principle which they think is essential to their welfare.

CHAPTER V.

Trades Unions and Strikes.

IN my previous remarks, I have endeavoured to make you distinctly perceive that wages are regulated by demand and supply. The employers and employed are just as much parties to a bargain, as are the buyers and the sellers of any commodity. It therefore seems to me that the one fundamental question to be decided with regard to strikes, is simply this: Is the combination which a Strike implies necessary, in order that the labourer may have the same chance of selling his labour dearly as the master has of buying this labour cheaply? If it can be proved that without strikes the working man would not be able to obtain the best price for his labour, I think strikes at once become justifiable. If, on the other hand, it can be proved that as high wages would be paid if strikes were never resorted to, the conclusion cannot then be resisted that a strike is an unmitigated evil.

I have stated the issue to be determined in as simple language as possible, because the discussion of this subject is often confused by the introduction of many collateral topics. Thus most people decide beforehand, that a strike implies everything that is bad, because they assume that a strike is never carried on, without resorting to physical violence and unjustifiable coercion. I am quite prepared to admit that the leaders of a strike have not unfrequently been guilty of gross cruelty and injustice towards those who refuse to join the combination. The builders' operatives of London who struck for higher wages in 1860, often attempted to use physical force against those who wished to continue working. In Sheffield, trade outrages have often assumed the form of dastardly murders, and explosive bombs have been cast into the houses of those who refused to submit to some regulation, which a section of some of their fellow working men were anxious to enforce. But such acts as these cannot fairly be regarded as the inevitable consequences of combinations being formed amongst working men; these acts of violence are illegal, and those who commit them ought to receive the most severe punishment the law can inflict. But experience has shown that the largest combinations of working men have often been formed without the slightest coercion

of individuals, and without doing anything which
even bore the semblance of illegality.   In order to
corroborate this opinion, I would particularly refer
to the great Preston Strike of 1854.   Seventeen
thousand cotton operatives then struck for an
advance of 10 per cent. in their wages; not one
single individual was coerced to join this strike;
the vast combination was the result of a voluntary
effort.   The strike continued during thirty-six
weeks.   The rigour of a severe winter increased
the hardships that were endured.   No complaints
were heard, no violence was attempted, but these
poor creatures bore their sufferings with a calm
resignation, and with a noble heroism, which even
those who were bitterly opposed to strikes con-
fessed were worthy of a better cause.   Numerous
other examples could be quoted, which would still
further corroborate the opinion, that a strike has
often been simply a peaceful and voluntary combination, and when such is the case, no one can
pretend that working men have not a clear and
undoubted right to join a strike.   Individual freedom would cease to exist, if every man had
not the most complete liberty to decide whether he should or should not work for the
wages which were offered to him.   For similar reasons, a number of working men have an indisputable right to join in an unanimous determina-

tion not to work for the wages which are offered
to them.

If the manufacturers in any particular district
believed that they were selling their goods too
cheaply, no one could blame them, if they agreed
amongst themselves not to sell any more goods
until the price advanced. These manufacturers
would however act very foolishly, if in the end
they should discover that the price which they had
declined was the full price, and that consequently
no higher price could be secured after a heavy loss
had been incurred by withholding their goods from
sale, perhaps for many months. Since the manufacturers have a perfect right to do what they
like with their goods, those whom they employ
have an equal right not to sell their labour, if they
think it realises too small a price. The goods
which the manufacturers keep unsold, represent so
much capital remaining idle, but they suppose
that the increase of price which will ultimately be
secured, will compensate them for the profit which
this capital would have yielded if productively
employed. In the same way, the labourers suppose
that an ultimate advance in wages will recompense
them for the loss of wages which they suffer
during the time they are on strike. I have already
said that the manufacturers would do a very
foolish thing if they acted upon wrong calculations,

and were unable at last to obtain a higher price for the goods which they wished to sell. The labourers would exhibit equal folly if they made wrong calculations, and were thus unable in the end to secure an advance in wages; for they would have suffered great pecuniary loss, and would have probably endured much physical hardship, without achieving the slightest compensating advantage. The points therefore which we must decide are these: Can a strike ever exert any influence in advancing wages? If not, a strike must be condemned as a most pernicious economic fallacy. If, on the other hand, it can be proved that in certain circumstances a strike may succeed in raising wages, we must carefully inquire what these circumstances are, in order to establish some principles to guide the labourers.

In attempting to supply an answer to the first of these two questions, it is necessary to revert briefly to the circumstances which determine the amount of wages received by any class of labourers. It has already been remarked that with regard to each separate industry, there is at any time a certain rate of profit, and also a certain rate of wages, which may be regarded as the natural rate. Thus one branch of industry may involve a greater risk than another, and therefore on the average of years, a larger rate of profit must be realised, in order that a compensation may be obtained for the additional risk incurred. Again, some classes of labourers always receive higher wages than others. For instance, some employment may require particular skill; some workmen are only employed a part of the year; some kinds of labour are more dangerous and unhealthy than others; these and various other circumstances which have been enumerated in a previous lecture, cause permanently different rates of wages to prevail in different employments.

I think it will be admitted, that neither the employers nor the employed can have any just ground of complaint, if in the particular industry in which they are jointly engaged, the natural rate of profit, as well as the natural rate of wages are both secured; for this result can be only brought about when the law of demand and supply has had free and unrestrained operation. Let us as an example suppose, that in the cotton trade at some particular time, a profit of fifteen per cent. upon the aggregate capital invested, represents the natural rate of profit, and that twenty shillings a week paid to the able-bodied spinner represents the natural rate of wages. It is easy to show that as long as this industry remains in the position just described, it would be vain to attempt to raise wages by any combination; for if wages were raised, the profits of the employer would be diminished; and I have assumed that he was previously obtaining just the requisite amount of profit to remunerate him for interest, for labour of superintendence, and for risk against loss; if therefore his profits were diminished, he would be placed in an unfavourable position compared with other employers, and capital would consequently be gradually withdrawn from this particular industry, and therefore a smaller amount would be distributed in wages. Hence it appears that any attempt to raise wages by diminishing profits below the natural rate cannot be successful, and will most probably cause a very serious permanent injury to the labourers. For employers who withdraw capital from their business, because their profits are unduly depressed by an unnatural rise in wages, may not again invest this capital, and thus the prosperity of the particular industry may be permanently diminished. I think therefore it has been conclusively proved, that when a trade is in a steady condition, or in other words, when both the natural rate of profit is realised, and the natural rate of wages is obtained, any attempt to raise wages must be either futile, or will in all probability be very injurious to the labourers themselves. When the truth of this last proposition has been admitted, writers on strikes usually argue in the following way. They say, and no doubt with perfect truth, that there is a tendency constantly in operation to bring each trade into a state which we have described as steady; for profits and wages are constantly approximating towards the natural rate. These writers then not unfrequently assume, that a principle has been enunciated, from which it can be at once demonstrated that a strike can never exert any effect in raising wages. They seek to substantiate this opinion by adopting the following line of argument. If wages cannot be raised above their natural rate without diminishing profits below their natural rate, and if profits and wages in every branch of industry are constantly approximating towards the natural rate, it follows as a necessary inference that a strike cannot raise wages, because the rise in wages would imply a reduction of profits below the natural rate; this is a result which has been proved to be unattainable.

The above reasoning, though apparently so plausible, involves an important fallacy. The argument would be conclusive, if profits and wages in any employment were always exactly at the natural rate. But it has only been affirmed that profits and wages are constantly approximating to their natural rate. The force of gravity never ceases to exert a tendency to restore the moving pendulum to a position of equilibrium. The pendulum may however be acted on by disturbing forces, which may cause it to deviate greatly from this position of equilibrium. In a similar way, demand and supply may be regarded as a force which is constantly tending to make wages and profits attain a natural rate; disturbing causes may however temporarily produce a great divergence from this natural rate, and we must therefore enquire whether during the period that is required to restore the wages and profits of any industry to their natural rate, such a combination as a strike implies, can succeed in securing a higher remuneration for the labourer.

Reverting to the illustration already given, we will assume that the cotton trade has been for some time in a steady state; the profits of the employer are 15 per cent., and wages are so adjusted that the able-bodied spinner receives one pound a week. Both the employers and the employed are satisfied, since each party to the bargain obtains exactly what is his due. Let it now however be supposed that this trade becomes suddenly extremely prosperous. Some foreign country may perhaps have repealed a prohibitory tariff; a new market for cotton goods may be thus created; the demand for these goods will consequently be increased, and their price will rapidly advance. Under such circumstances, the profits of the employer may at once be even doubled or trebled. The employers can therefore now afford to pay higher wages, and the question arises, Will the labourer by entering into a combination secure a larger portion of the additional profits, which his master obtains in periods of active trade? Various arguments may be advanced on each side of the question; I will proceed to state them as briefly and as candidly as I can. On the one hand it may no doubt be urged, that wages are always regulated by demand and supply, and that therefore it must be futile to endeavour to increase them beyond the point which would be attained by the natural operation of demand and supply. In support of this opinion, experience may be appealed to, in order to show that when any particular branch of industry becomes extremely profitable, those engaged in it are sure to receive higher wages. For instance, during the two or three years which preceded the Civil War in America, the cotton trade of Lancashire was in a state of unprecedented prosperity. The profits were so immense, that large fortunes were rapidly accumulated by the manufacturers. It is however well known that the operatives participated in this prosperity, and that much greater wages were paid to them than they had

ever before been accustmed to receive. During
this period, no rumour of a strike was ever heard;
and it may therefore be thought to be conclusively
proved, that a strike can exert no influence in
advancing wages during periods of active trade.
But before we accept this conclusion, let us consider what really occurs under the circumstances
supposed.   It is too often forgotten that those who
are engaged as employers in any particular business,
virtually form themselves in each district into a
combination, for the express purpose of regulating
wages.   Go to Manchester, Halifax, Bradford, or
Belfast, and you will find in each of these towns,
the operatives are paid for the work done, according to a uniform scale of remuneration.   You may
often have observed in the public prints, that the
cotton manufacturers have held a meeting in Manchester, and have unanimously agreed to a certain
alteration in wages; and every employer in the
district at once adopts either the reduction or
the advance, which has been agreed upon at this
meeting. The same thing occurs in other branches
of industry. The proprietors of collieries hold a
meeting, at which they decide to alter the wages
they shall pay, and the alteration is immediately
accepted by every colliery owner in the district.
Sometimes the same object is not less effectually
attained, although the combination does not take

the significant form of a public meeting. Thus
the same kind of agricultural work may be very
differently remunerated in Yorkshire and Dorsetshire; but in the same locality, and within a certain area a uniform rate of agricultural wages
almost invariably prevails. Farmers when they
meet at market talk over what they shall pay
for particular kinds of work, and you will find
that a certain fixed price is at length agreed upon
for reaping, mowing, hoeing, &c. We must therefore consider whether the labourers who may be
regarded as one party to a bargain, can safely
trust the terms of this bargain to a combination
of employers. I believe it can be easily shewn
that the labourer is placed at a disadvantage, if
he attempts simply as an individual to arrange
this bargain, and I further believe that labourers
must show that they have the power of combining,
in order at all times to be able to sell their labour
on the best possible terms.

With the view of substantiating the opinion
which has just been expressed, I will suppose that
there has been a marked improvement in the cotton
trade; the profits of the manufacturers are greatly
increased; they consequently agree to make a
general advance in wages of 10 per cent. Those
whom they employ may feel that this advance
is not sufficient, and that their masters from their

additional profits could well afford to make an
advance in wages of 20 per cent. Operatives in
their individual capacity express their dissatisfac-
tion. *A*, *B*, or *C* may go to his employer and
say, I think you are not paying me sufficient
wages. The employer replies, that he and his
brother manufacturers have unanimously decided
what wages they shall pay, and if any of their
workmen are not contented with the remuneration
that is offered to them, they are of course at
perfect liberty to discontinue working. The operative knows that further contention is useless; his
master will not be induced to swerve from his
determination by an isolated protest, and therefore the operative is compelled to accept what is
offered to him, or else to relinquish his employment, because since wages are fixed on a uniform
scale, it is vain for him to expect to obtain more
from any other manufacturer. But let us see how
the case would be altered, if the workmen formed
themselves into a great combination and adopted
united action. It was plainly proved by the Preston strike, that such a combination can be formed;
for then, all the operatives in a large district were
unanimous in their determination not to work,
unless their wages were advanced 10 per cent.,
and this resolution was unwaveringly adhered to
during thirty-six weeks. When such a combina-

tion is formed, the leaders of the movement would no longer speak to their employers as individuals, representing no authority, and therefore possessing no power, but they would then express the fixed resolve of combined thousands. They might then say to their employers, We place two alternatives before you; you must either accept our demands, or you will be left without labour, and your mills will be for a long time closed. If the employers felt that they could afford to yield that which was asked, it would be in all probability granted, rather than incur the loss of being compelled temporarily to discontinue their business. Each party in the dispute of course ought to feel, that the contest on which they were embarked, involved the most serious consequences. The employers if they were compelled to suspend their business would have an immense amount of capital which before was highly remunerative, at once made unproductive. On the other hand, the employed would if their demands were refused be deprived of their daily subsistence, and in order to support themselves when thrown out of work, they would be obliged to spend those savings which had required years to accumulate. We are free to confess that these melancholy results have accompanied every strike. The losses which have been inflicted upon the employer have often seriously diminished his capital, and his capital forms the fund from which wages are supplied. The employed moreover have not only spent their own savings, but have drawn largely from their fellow workmen in other parts of the country; and those who, when in receipt of their ordinary wages are accustomed to live in comparative comfort, have been often compelled to endure the greatest privations. During the Preston strike, the operatives were reduced almost to a state of starvation, and they no doubt suffered the most terrible hardships.

It might seem, that if these are the sad results of a strike, all combinations on the part of the employed ought to be condemned, although an occasional advance in wages may be obtained from such combinations. I know that upon such considerations the question is usually decided. It is said that the workmen are almost always unsuccessful in their strikes, and that this will continue to be the case, because the employers, although their capital remains idle, do not really suffer a tithe part as many privations as must be borne by the employed when they are thrown out of work. In order still further to prove that a strike never ought to be resorted to, a comparison is made between those strikes in which the workmen have failed, and those in which they have succeeded, and it is shown that a heavy aggregate loss is on the side of the workmen. I am fully prepared to admit that this loss is really much greater than it is usually represented to be ; the labourers not only lose the wages which they would receive if they were at work, but as we have before said, the great cost which a strike entails upon the master, also ultimately falls to a certain extent upon the labourer ; because it diminishes the capital from which the wages of the labourers are paid. It seems to me however that a calculation of the outlay which strikes necessitate, affords no assistance in determining the real influence which they exert upon the condition of the labourer. Costly armaments are maintained in order to give security to life and property, and it would be a fallacious argument to say, that the millions which our army and navy annually cost represent a useless expenditure ; they are useful because it is owing to them that no foreign power dares to make a hostile attack against us. When we once embark in war, the most complete triumph will give no immediate pecuniary compensation for the immense expenditure which the contest has required. The chief reward which a nation obtains from carrying on a just and successful war, arises from the circumstance that peace is in future more effectually secured, for foreign nations are made to understand the power which will be brought against them, if they do any international wrong either towards life or property.   In a similar way, I think it can be shown that a strike, although its immediate consequences may be terrible, yet may exert a powerful influence to place the future relations between employers and employed on a more peaceful and a more satisfactory basis.

As an example, the great Preston Strike of 1854, unmistakably demonstrated to the masters, that the employed possess so complete a power of combination, that all the operatives in a large district can for many weeks keep firmly to the resolution, that they will refuse to work unless certain conditions are granted.   If therefore, the masters can really afford to do what is asked of them, I think that they are more likely to grant the concession, when they know what sad disasters a refusal would bring, both to themselves and to the employed.   I have been assured by one of the prominent leaders of this strike, that since this great contest has been fought, everything has gone on most comfortably between the employers and the employed.   Each party feels what the other will do as a last resource; the operatives every year becoming more intelligent by improved education, carefully watch the price of the raw material and the price of manufactured goods, and are thus enabled to form an

accurate estimate of their masters' profits. The
employers assume that the employed possess this
knowledge. When trade is good and profits increase, a fair and reasonable advance in wages is
immediately made, and joyfully accepted; when
trade is bad and profits decline, wages are reduced ;
the reduction is looked upon as necessary, and is
therefore borne without murmur or complaint. In
times gone by, the relations between employers
and employed were perhaps more unsatisfactory in
the cotton trade than in any other industry. A
feeling of rancour and distrust existed between
masters and men, dastardly acts of violence were
sometimes resorted to, and a feeling of revenge
not unfrequently prompted the destruction of the
employers' property. But the Preston Strike of
1854 was a great struggle, which taught each
party in the conflict the other's power, and in this
way peace seems for the future to have been effectually secured; for since that time, although the
cotton trade has been characterised by the greatest
prosperity, and by an unprecedented adversity,
yet there has been no rumour of a strike; there
scarcely appears to have been even the semblance
of a dispute between masters and men. In 1858—9,
when the masters were realising enormous gains,
wages were advanced, and the operatives were satisfied with the additional remuneration which was

thus offered to them. When the Civil War commenced in America, the customary supply of raw cotton was so much diminished, that the whole trade was completely paralysed; wages were reduced, and manufactories were closed. A vast multitude were thrown out of work; and those men who before were comparatively affluent were suddenly reduced to a state of abject misery; their savings, which had been accumulated by a life's toil, were soon exhausted, and the charity of the whole nation had to be appealed to, in order to keep them from starvation. But these sufferings, terrible as they were, were borne with a calm resignation, and with a noble heroism, which has made those who perhaps suspected the political and social aspirations of our working men, anticipate a glorious future for our country.

Briefly summarising the opinions which I have expressed on the subject, I think that the labourers by showing that they have the power of forming combinations, place themselves in a position which enables them to obtain the best price for their labour. When employers recognise the existence of this power of combination, they will be careful to advance their wages immediately they can afford to do so; and they will not reduce wages, until bad trade compels them to take this step. The advantage which the labourers might thus obtain would, I conceive, be most dearly purchased, if it was necessary frequently to resort to strikes, in order to exhibit this power of combination. I have, however, adduced the Preston Strike, as a proof that a strike on a large scale, soon causes this power of combination to be generally recognised, and therefore a strike may be conceived as a temporary evil, because it seems to create a guarantee against its future recurrence. I am however free to confess that the leaders of a strike, in assuming an attitude of hostility to their employers, are usually misled by the most pernicious economic fallacies. They talk wildly about the oppression of capital, and the tyranny of competition; but let us not deal too harshly with them; if we think they are wrong, let us try calmly to reason with them, and to teach them the truth; for we must remember that those who were the most educated, and those who were supposed to be the most intelligent amongst us, have professed their belief in economic fallacies as glaring and perhaps more mischievous than any which have been uttered by an agitator for a strike. Not twenty years since, some of the most intellectual men in this country, our greatest statesmen, our leading writers, thought that our national industry could not exist, unless it was defended by a protective tariff. The advantages of Free Trade are now so generally admitted that at

the present time a protectionist would be laughed
to scorn.   In a similar way, working men are gradually becoming more enlightened on economic
questions.   The day is not perhaps far distant,
when they will indulge in no more rash talk against
capital and competition.   We may hope that they
will soon understand, that capital is the fund from
which the wages are paid, and that they are
therefore benefited by any circumstance which
tends to increase capital.   Moreover, competition
does not reduce wages; for when competition is
active, employers compete as actively for labour,
as labourers compete for work, and thus each individual is more likely to sell his labour for exactly
what it is worth.

It has been already stated, that in the great
majority of strikes, the workmen have failed to
secure the object which they sought.   The cause of
their failure is, no doubt, often due to the superior
strength which the employers in such a conflict
possess, on account of their greater resources.
Wealthy manufacturers incur a heavy loss, if they
are compelled to close their mills during many
weeks; but the loss which is thus inflicted upon
them, bears no comparison with the sufferings which
the labourers are obliged to endure.   It may therefore be reasonably supposed, that in so unequal a
conflict, victory is most frequently with the strong.

But the labourers cannot attribute the repeated failure of their strikes solely to the inferiority of their resources. The erroneous opinions which they entertain concerning the causes which regulate wages, often induce them to commence a strike, in order to obtain an object, which neither in justice nor reason, the employers can be expected to grant. When a strike is commenced, the labourers do not usually stay to inquire whether their employers can afford to grant what is demanded from them; but the language which is ordinarily employed on these occasions is, that it is unjust that wages should be reduced, or that the same wages ought to be paid for a smaller number of hours of work. It should be borne in mind, that it implies a fundamental misconception to speak of wages being just or unjust; it would be not less idle to speak of the justice or injustice of a particular price being charged for bread; if bread is made dear by artificial restrictions, then it is right that these restrictions should be repealed; but when the dearness is due to a natural scarcity of corn, we must endeavour to remedy the evil by making corn more plentiful. In the same way if wages are reduced, because the profits of the employer are diminishing, or because the supply of labour is increasing; it is no use talking about justice or injustice, for the evil can be cured only

by improving the trade, or by diminishing the
supply of labour. It is most important that the
labourers should never lose sight of the great truth,
that wages are not controlled by abstract justice;
but wages are regulated by causes, which are as
certain in their operation, as are the physical forces
which govern nature. If labourers more generally
understood these economic truths, strikes would
not be so frequently resorted to, in order to obtain
what the labourers have no valid reason to claim.
I have already admitted their undoubted right
fairly to participate in the additional profits which
their employers might obtain ; they are also clearly
justified in resisting a reduction of wages, if they
believe that there is no decline in profits to war-
rant labour being worse remunerated. We have
however again and again insisted, that the remuneration of the labourer is ultimately regulated by
demand and supply; and that a tendency exists,
although time may be required to complete its
operation, to make the wages and profits of every
employment approximate to the natural rate. It
may therefore be always reasonably concluded, that
both the natural rate of wages, and also the natural rate of profit prevail in a trade, if for some
time nothing has occurred to produce any sudden variation in the returns realised from it.

Let us suppose that some particular employ-

ment, say the building trade, is in this position;
and that those who are employed in it suddenly
become impressed with the conviction, that they
are working too many hours for the wages which
they receive. This was the point at issue in the
late great strike* amongst the building operatives
of London. I refer to this strike, because it happened that for a time, I was somewhat intimately
connected with the operatives, who were deputed
by their fellow-workmen to be their leaders and
their spokesmen. It is hardly necessary to remind
you, that almost all our leading newspapers at
once assumed, that the operatives were entirely in
error. The leaders of the strike were denounced
day after day in the most violent terms, for their
ignorance of the first principles of economic science;
and the general body of the supporters of the
strike were commiserated as being poor deluded
creatures, who were influenced by designing agita-
tors. I recalled to mind, that we in the middle and
upper classes have often professed opinions, which
showed a complete ignorance of the principles
of economic science. I therefore thought it was
unfair to blame those for their want of knowledge, who have much less time for study than
ourselves. It seemed to me to be our duty to

* This strike occurred in the early spring of 1860.

endeavour to instruct, rather than to blame. I therefore ventured to ask the men who were on strike to
meet me in a large public room in London, and
I told them that I would try to place the question
before them in its true economic aspects. When
addressing them on the subject, I was scrupulously
careful, to point out to them how extremely fallacious were many of the opinions which they expressed. Although I attacked many of their most
fondly cherished prejudices, yet their demeanour
indicated, that they were sincerely desirous to be
instructed. The point which I chiefly endeavoured
to urge upon them was this, You demand the
same wages for less work ; you have no right to
make this demand, unless you can show, that circumstances have recently occurred to increase your
masters' profits ; for unless a trade is suddenly improved by exceptional causes, the competition of
capital insures that the profits realized shall closely
approximate, to what has been described as the
natural rate. If you compel your employers to
reduce their profits below this natural rate, by
increasing your wages, you will be really doing
yourselves far more harm than good; for capital
is withdrawn from a business when it does not
realise the ordinary rate of profit, and you will
attract more labourers to your trade, if you create
an artificial advance in your wages. You may there-

fore bring into operation two circumstances which
will ultimately injure you; because, in the first
place, you may diminish the capital which forms
the fund which is distributed in wages amongst
you; and, in the second place, you may increase
the number of those, amongst whom this fund is
to be distributed. I therefore urge you, for your
own sakes, not to act in this matter without calm
reflection. It would no doubt be a happy circumstance if your hours of toil could be shortened.
The marvellous increase in the production of
national wealth, cannot be a subject for much
congratulation, until it can be shown that this
greater wealth is so distributed, that the labourer
can more frequently cease from his toil either to
enjoy the pleasures of mind, or to admire the
glories which a bounteous nature has spread around
him. But anxious as we may be to see the hours
of toil shortened, yet we must remember that the
remuneration of labour is regulated by certain definite causes. If labour is made more efficient, masters and men may both receive a greater reward.
But if the employed attempt to augment their own
gains by unduly reducing the profits of their employers, capital will be withdrawn from business,
and a source of employment may be thus permanently closed. The builders' strike may be
regarded as suggesting one happy omen, for it

seems to indicate, that the labourers will henceforth be anxious to appropriate each advance of wages to a reduction of the hours of their daily toil.

I have already remarked, that people generally suppose that unmixed harm must always result from a strike. When considering such a subject, I often call to mind the words of our great poet, who says,

> There is a soul of goodness in things evil,
> Would men observingly distil it out.

If there is any truth in the views which I have expressed, it is not difficult to see that there is a " soul of goodness" beneath all the rancour and the suffering which are the usual concomitants of a strike. I have striven to show that, when working men possess the power of combined action, they participate more readily and more certainly in the prosperity and adversity of the particular industry, in which they may happen to be employed. If profits increase, an advance of wages is at once insured to them ; and if profits are depressed below the ordinary rate, they will recognise the necessity of immediately submitting to a reduction in their wages. But if these are the relations which are made to subsist between employers and employed, is there not a copartnership created between them ?

for when there is a copartnership, the aggregate remuneration received by the labourer depends partly upon the profits which his master obtains. The great defect in our present national economy arises from the fact, that between employers and employed there is no common pecuniary interest ; an antagonism of feeling is thus often engendered; they strive against each other like hostile parties, higgling over a bargain. The efficiency of our industry is thus most seriously impeded, because capital and labour ought cordially to cooperate upon the work, which cannot be accomplished without their united action. It is evident that this serious defect in our national economy would be to a great extent remedied, if copartnerships between employers and employed were more frequent. I therefore think it has been shown, that strikes have at least one happy and beneficial tendency, because since they make labourers participate in the prosperity and adversity of the capitalist, they must also tend to create a copartnership between masters and men. Important as may be the good which would be thus effected, other results might ultimately follow, of still higher consequence to the wellbeing of our labouring population. Such a copartnership as has been here described, would so train and educate the labourers, as to enable them with a certainty of

success to conduct Cooperative Trading Societies.
A copartnership would make the labourers more
intimately acquainted with the management of
a business; they would gradually learn to understand the various circumstances which con-
tribute to make any industry successful; they
would have practically taught to them the various functions which capital performs; they
would soon see how essential it was that the
managers of each department should be able
men, and that implicit obedience should be paid
to their authority. It would also soon be discovered, that in almost every branch of industry
there are great fluctuations in the returns; good
years in which large profits are realised being
often succeeded by bad years, in which scarcely
any profit is obtained. These truths must be
known by the labourers, before cooperation, applied to trade, can achieve any general success.

You will observe that the title given to this lecture is, "The Influence exerted by Trades Unions
and Strikes." As yet little has been said about
Trades Unions, but as the two subjects have been
grouped together, I must try to explain to you
whether or not, there is any necessary connection
between a Trades Union and a Strike. A trades
union, as its name implies, is a society composed
of working men; and each of these societies com-

prises only those who are employed in some particular business, or in some special department of
the business. Thus masons, carpenters, hatters,
gas-fitters, in fact, almost every class of labourers,
have their own trades union. It often happens
that in the case of a restricted branch of industry, such as wool-sorting, all those who are
employed in it, in different parts of the country,
belong to one central society, the management of
which is in London. But when the industry is
more extensive, numbers of these societies are
established in different parts of the country. For
instance, the masons in almost every large town
have a trades union of their own, which as far as
management is concerned, is independent of any
central authority. A certain correspondence is
kept up between these different societies, and
occasionally they may consult together as to the
course of action which ought to be adopted in
certain junctures. But the masons who belong to
a trades union at Plymouth would not consider
themselves to be in the least degree bound to
demand higher wages, although the masons of a
trades union in Glasgow, in order to obtain this
object may consider themselves justified, in resorting to a strike. There always exists a certain
feeling of sympathy between the workmen in the
same employment who happen to belong to a

trade society; and if, for instance, the masons who were union-men happened to be on strike in one locality, their fellow unionists in other parts of the country would almost feel it their duty to assist them by subscriptions. The trades unionists in other employments frequently support those who are on strike. It has, for instance, been calculated, that no less a sum than £20,000 was sent by working men to the Preston operatives who were engaged in the great strike of 1854.

Trades Unions are almost invariably denounced, because it is erroneously supposed, that the only object they seek to attain is to supply an organization which will enable labourers to enter into combinations. It should be remembered that some of the most important functions which these societies perform, are either prudential or charitable. Thus each member of a trades union subscribes so much a week to a common fund, and in return for this, an amount is each week paid to him if he is thrown out of employment, either by dullness of trade, or by illness. When the member of a trade society dies, his family often receives a certain sum to defray the cost of the funeral, and to cover other expenses which may have been incurred during his illness. Hence a trades union effects all the objects which are sought to be obtained by friendly societies. Such societies when well managed, are regarded as most excellent institutions ; and, as a general rule, the funds of a trades union are administered with strict integrity. But to the Political Economist the most curious and most important point to be considered in connection with trades unions, is the effect which is exerted upon industry by the rules which these societies enforce upon their members. Some of these rules may be regarded simply as trade regulations. Thus it sometimes happens, that a member of a trades union is not permitted to take more than a certain number of apprentices, and only one of his own sons can be apprenticed to the trade. In some cases the members of these societies are obliged to do their work in a particular way. Thus it was alleged by the employers, although it was denied by the men, that the bricklayers were ordered by their unions to adopt a certain method in laying their bricks, whereas, if they had been laid in a different manner the work would have been more quickly and better done. Again, it has frequently happened, that the members of these societies will not continue to work if a certain machine is used, the employment of which they erroneously suppose will be detrimental to the labourer. Before we inquire into the policy or impolicy, and into the justice or injustice of these rules, we will consider how the power is

13

obtained, which gives these rules their authority. In some branches of industry the trades unions, so far as the labourers are concerned, are omnipotent. I believe there is not a single person employed in the wool-stapling business who is not a Union man. When a trades union is in this position it is not difficult to maintain its authority. The majority becomes supreme, for if any master employed a non-union man, all his other workmen who belonged to the union would immediately refuse to remain in his employment. Hence this question arises, Are the labourers justified in pursuing this course of conduct, and are they really benefited by it? They do nothing illegal as long as they refrain from all acts of physical violence. Sometimes however they endeavour forcibly to coerce those who will not join their union; sometimes also, they destroy the property of those who insist on employing non-union men. But in these instances, an offence is committed, which we should all hope to see punished with the utmost rigour of the law. For such social tyranny exercised by the majority over the minority ought to be regarded as one of the most detestable kinds of oppression. It must however be acknowledged that such offences, which are now known as trade outrages, are confined to a few localities, and that those who perpetrate them are vehemently denounced by the general body of trades unionists. Sheffield has obtained an unenviable notoriety for the dreadful trade outrages which have been committed in that town. It has more than once happened that a file grinder, because he refused to join the union, has had a destructive bomb thrown into his house, or has had his grinding machine filled with some explosive material, the explosion of which will endanger his life. This abominable tyranny has become almost unbearable, and if it is continued, Sheffield may not improbably lose some of its most important manufactures. Large steel works have already been established at Manchester, and it has been stated that Manchester was selected, in preference to Sheffield, in consequence of trade outrages being so prevalent at the latter place.

I have already said, that trades unionists rarely do any act which can be regarded as illegal; but they maintain and exercise their authority, by exerting an influence which often bears too much the character of social oppression. Those who refuse to join the union are subject to a great variety of petty annoyances and slights, which, though difficult to describe, yet may make a life very miserable. You can best conceive what has to be borne, by imagining what a barrister would suffer, if he should do anything which his fellow-barristers

might consider as unprofessional. He would not
be permitted to dine at the bar mess; some of the
leading members of the bar would perhaps refuse
to hold briefs with him; and by resorting to these
forms of social punishment, the bar is enabled to
enforce as much obedience to their rules, as if these
rules had a legal sanction. It is curious to remark,
that the rules to which the members of trades
unions are bound to pay obedience, are, in many
respects, similar to those which regulate the conduct of the members of the legal profession. Thus,
a barrister is not permitted to appear in court for
less than a certain fee; and a trade unionist is not
permitted to do a particular kind of work, unless
he receives a certain remuneration. Again, no at-
torney can have more than two articled pupils. It
may, on the one hand, be maintained that such a
restriction is necessary, in order that every member
of the profession may be properly taught; but, on
the other hand, it may with some reason be urged
that the real object of such a restriction is to limit
competition, with the view of augmenting the gains
of those engaged in the profession. In a similar
way, it is a rule of many trades unions, that no
workman should have under him at the same time
more than a fixed number of apprentices; and in
some employments, such as the wool trade, it is
ordered by the rules of the union, that a workman

should not bring up more than one son to his own trade. The workmen, in the same way as the law-yers, defend these regulations by maintaining that they are necessary in order to secure the efficiency of labour; for if the number of apprentices was not limited, labour would not be properly trained, work would be badly done, and thus the perma-nent prosperity of the industry might be jeopar-dised. Others may fairly take a different view, and may think that the real object sought to be obtained by limiting the number of apprentices is to restrict competition, and thus artificially raise the rate of wages by diminishing the supply of labour.

Any number of individuals, as long as they do not interfere with the perfect freedom of action of others, have an undoubted right to agree amongst themselves to be bound by a common code of laws. But I would earnestly ask the workmen calmly to consider, whether they are really doing justice to themselves, and whether they gain any sufficient advantage in sacrificing so much of their individuality. It certainly seems wrong, that a father should not be freely permitted to train his son to that particular employment, which his natu-ral endowments may best qualify him to follow. A man would feel in after life that a cruel injustice had been inflicted on him, if he had been prevented by the arbitrary regulations of trade-societies from engaging in those branches of industry in which nature had apparently destined him to achieve success. Mankind in general would suffer, if those who may be physically weak, but are gifted with delicacy of touch, are driven to pursue those kinds of labour which chiefly require muscular strength; whilst, at the same time, those who have the sturdy limb and the strong arm, are unnaturally forced into an industry which requires not strength, but the trained dexterity of hand and eye. Moreover, the labourers should remember that wealth is in England accumulated so rapidly, because in industry, we are able to compete successfully with the whole world. In many trades the competition is so keen and so close, that victory only just turns in our favour. The balance of advantage is so slightly on our side, that if we were hampered by many vexatious restrictions, other competitors would readily undersell us, and thus our foreign commerce might soon be imperilled. Sheffield has to contend against Liége, Manchester has to compete against Rouen and Mulhouse, and the silk manufacturers of England, although they have the advantage of cheap coal and admirable machinery, must not forget that their brethren in France can employ operatives who work for lower wages, and who seem to inherit a more exquisite taste for the

beauty of colour. If, therefore, the balance of advantage should even be turned slightly against us,
we may lose the advantage which we now possess,
and an industry which employs thousands of hands,
may gradually decay.

I have endeavoured, with as little prejudice as
possible, to discuss the influence exerted by trades
unions. I have shown that these societies often
perform a most important service, by enabling the
labourers to make a provision against any disasters
which may be brought upon them, either by illness,
or by the fluctuations of trade. I also trust that I
have been sufficiently explicit in warning the labourers against the impolicy and injustice of en-
forcing any arbitrary trade regulations, which may
either impede the successful prosecution of industry, or may coerce the individual freedom of those
who do not wish to join these trade combinations.
I have hitherto purposely avoided associating trades
unions with strikes, because it is generally erroneously assumed, that between trades unions and
strikes there is a necessary and an inevitable connection. The origin of this error may be easily
explained. A strike and a trades union both
imply a combination; but those who combine to
form a trades union, may never consent to allow
the combination which is thus formed, to supply
the organization which a strike requires. Many

working men are as much opposed to strikes as are their employers; and yet not a few of the working men who hold these opinions are members of trades unions. It is easy to understand how it comes to pass that these societies are so constantly connected with strikes; a strike requires combination; and a trades union always has, as it were, ready at hand the combination which a strike needs.

CHAPTER VI.

Emigration.

DURING the last few years, the present and future position of our labouring population has been most powerfully affected by emigration. Many of the circumstances which we have already discussed, are perhaps somewhat uncertain in their operation. Opinions may differ as to the consequences which would result, if a greater area of land was owned and cultivated by labourers, and if a greater portion of our national industry was carried on through the medium of co-operative institutions. No one, however, can deny the great influence which has already been produced upon the condition of our labourers by emigration; and if this emigration continues on a large scale during many years, the remuneration of labour may be so greatly increased as materially to affect not only the labourers, but also every other section of the community. Hitherto we have had a surplus population which has supplied with labour many countries which are gradu-

ally rising, or which have already risen into wealth
and prosperity. We have therefore accustomed
ourselves to consider emigration, without dwelling
upon the no less important effects which result
from an immigration of labour into a country.
Some nations have a population far more dense
than our own. China is peopled as thickly as it
can be, until its resources are developed with
greater skill and knowledge. The underpaid
Chinese labourer has already shown an anxiety
to leave his own country, in order to obtain the
large wages which are paid in Australia and California. It is therefore not an impossible supposition, that as labour becomes dearer in our own
country, we may witness a large immigration of
labour into England. I therefore hope to lay before you some of the many reflections which are
suggested, not only by emigration, but also by an
immigration of labour on a large scale.

At the beginning of this century, when Malthus
published his celebrated Essay on population, the
great social and economic problem which then required solution, was the relief of an over-stocked
labour market. The truth of the law was receiving
a sad and practical illustration, that as population
increases food becomes more expensive, unless a
greater demand for agricultural produce is met by
augmented importations, or by the introduction of

agricultural improvements. No pen can ever adequately describe the sufferings which our poor endured, at the period to which we are referring. Their
misery becomes the more deplorable to think upon,
when it is remembered that the cheap food which
was required was prevented from being sent to
these shores by protective duties, a policy which
remains a lasting monument, of either the ignorance,
or the selfishness of those who then governed the
State. If seasons were unpropitious, our own de-
ficient harvest could not be supplemented by supplies from other countries where the crop might
have been more abundant, until corn advanced almost to a famine price. Men then seemed born to
be a burden to themselves, and to everyone else
around them. During the winter months, great
numbers of able-bodied agricultural and other labourers, in vain endeavoured to obtain employment,
and they were obliged to live on the parish rates,
in order to avoid starvation. With a view of les-
sening the pecuniary burdens which such wide-
spread pauperism entailed, various expedients were
resorted to, which in many respects only aggravated
the misery of the poor. Employers, not unreason-
ably feared, that if workmen should be attracted to
a particular district by a sudden demand for labour,
they would remain there to swell the surplus population of the locality, if industry should again

become inactive. Various laws were consequently passed with the avowed object of preventing labourers from moving from the locality in which they were born. These various regulations, which were termed the laws of settlement, inflicted the greatest hardship upon the labourers, because they were prevented from seeking employment in those districts where the highest wages were paid.

But bad as was the condition of the labouring classes of England, it was infinitely worse in Ireland. In no civilised country has the mass of the people ever existed in more abject misery. And yet Ireland has natural resources well adapted for the production of great wealth. It is idle, in fact, it is almost wicked to explain Ireland's misfortunes, by saying that the Celtic is naturally inferior to the Saxon race. Ireland has produced soldiers, orators, statesmen, and thinkers, who have added lustre to the history of our empire. Moreover, the people who grovel in the huts of Tipperary at once possess so many industrial virtues, when they can labour under favourable economic conditions, that they have become the pioneers of civilisation in the Western world, and have there been the chief founders of nations which seem likely to rival us in wealth and prosperity. In Ireland, everything apparently combined to lower the condition of the people. Those who owned the land were absentee landlords, who never performed one of the duties which ought to attach to the possession of property. The land was let to peasant farmers, who were termed cottiers; they possessed no capital, except a few rude tools and the scanty furniture of their miserable dwellings. They cared not what rent they offered to pay; their only object was to obtain possession of a plot of ground; for they knew that however much they became indebted to their landlord, they had no property which he could seize, and that he must leave them sufficient potatoes to enable them to subsist. They had no motive to be industrious, or to exercise any prudence, for if they produced anything beyond a bare subsistence, it would be taken from them to pay their arrears of rent. They consequently married with the utmost recklessness, and the land, since no capital was applied to its cultivation, gradually became more and more impoverished. Since the population constantly increased, and, at the same time, the soil was more and more exhausted, the mass of the people sank deeper and deeper into the depths of abject poverty. In the year 1847 all this misery accumulated into a terrible crisis. The potato, which had become almost the sole food of the people was diseased, and the nation was decimated by the most ter-

rible famine which has been witnessed in modern
times.   There was not enough food in the
country to provide a bare subsistence, and one of
two alternatives became inevitable.   The people
must either starve or leave their country; the tens
of thousands who died from starvation can never
be accurately enumerated; and an emigration
commenced on such a gigantic scale from Ireland
to America, as can be only compared to the exodus
which is described in Holy Writ.   This emigration
soon acquired an accumulating intensity, for these
emigrants settled in the United States, where
fertile land was cheap, and where labour was highly
remunerated; their whole habit of life was changed.
Those who had been made improvident by hopeless wretchedness soon showed that they had the
virtues of prudence now that they had an opportunity of accumulating wealth.   The first object
to which they devoted their savings was to send
money back to Ireland, to enable all their relations
and friends to emigrate.   The amount thus remit-
ted between 1847 and 1864 has been not less
than £10,000,000; no statistical fact is more astonishing or more instructive. In this way emigration
has been so powerfully stimulated, that in twenty
years, from 1841 to 1861, the population of Ireland
was reduced from 8,100,000 to 5,800,000.   This
emigration must be regarded as a most happy

circumstance; for if it had not occurred, a great part of the nation must have fallen victims to all the horrors of starvation. It cannot however be denied, that the events which have occurred during these few years, form a mournful epoch in the history of our nation. It is not unfrequently asserted that Political Economy is a hard-hearted science; but in Ireland, everything was disregarded, which according to Political Economy would promote the production of wealth; and the result was, that it became absolutely necessary that the nation should be depopulated, either by starvation, or by emigration. If a retributive Providence governs the destinies of nations, we ought to feel that we must in future do much by thought and deed, to prevent the wrongs which Ireland has suffered from being avenged on those, who have misruled and mismanaged that country. I almost shudder when I sometimes hear the Irish opprobriously described as low, ignorant, and indolent; it is like cruelly thrusting a daughter into the streets, who has naturally noble instincts, and generous sentiments, and then upbraiding her because she becomes an outcast of society. Our sovereign would do well to take every opportunity of showing the most tender attention to the Irish, and thus try to soothe the memory of the many cruel wrongs which they have endured. Our legislature ought to be careful to discover whether in Ireland there are any abuses still to be remedied, which are the remnants of an oppression based on religious intolerance; and Irish landlords should strive by judicious liberality to make some amends for the wrongs which were committed in those days, when it seemed to be thought that there were rights, but no duties connected with the ownership of land.

The almost sudden reduction of the population from 8,000,000 to 6,000,000 has been a remedy, which, though severe, has nevertheless produced many happy results. The drafting away of this surplus population relieved the country from an onerous burden; the supply of labour of course became greatly lessened, and, as a consequence, wages have rapidly advanced. Previous to 1847 able bodied agricultural labourers in many parts of Ireland worked for fourpence a day, whereas now there is little difference between the wages paid in Ireland and in England. Formerly any additional demand for labour would cause thousands to flock from Ireland to England; our harvests were thus to a great extent reaped by labourers who came here from Ireland for two or three months in the year. But the number of labourers who leave Ireland for the English harvest has steadily diminished; and a very intelligent observer, who has lately travelled in that country assures me, that if the present rate of emigration from Ireland continues for some time longer, the day may not be far distant, when the Irish harvests will have to be reaped by English labourers. The reduction in the number of the labouring population has not been the only circumstance which has caused wages to advance in Ireland.

The sale of the property of embarrassed landowners has been so much facilitated in Ireland, that 2,800,000 acres, or one-seventh of the whole area of the island, has been sold in the Encumbered Estates Courts. The estates thus disposed of, were as a general rule possessed by those who were deeply in debt, and were consequently unable to carry out improvements; whereas the new proprietors are generally married men who have the requisite capital to secure efficient cultivation. Two causes have consequently combined to raise wages. In the first place, the number of the labouring population has decreased, and secondly capital, or in other words, the wage fund, has been augmented.

From England and Scotland during the last fifteen or twenty years, there has been a very large emigration, although the people have not been compelled to leave these countries by so sudden and awful a catastrophe, as that which

14

caused the Irish exodus. Our labourers did not emigrate in order to avert imminent starvation, but they left our shores with a view of improving their material condition, by settling in countries where labour was dear and land cheap. When we reflect on the pecuniary advantages which every emigrant may reasonably expect to obtain, it seems surprising that our labourers have not left us in much greater numbers. I have already endeavoured to show you that a large proportion of our working population are in a state of miserable poverty. The ordinary wages of our agricultural labourers are not more than nine or ten shillings a week; many of them live in dwellings which do not deserve the name of human habitations. It is scarcely possible for them to obtain the necessaries, much less any of the comforts of life. They cannot make any provision either for sickness or old age, and when their strength is exhausted by the hard toil which they have endured, they must bear the humiliation of becoming parish paupers. It seems wonderful that men who are in this condition, do not emigrate *en masse;* the United States, Australia and others of our colonies would gladly purchase their labour at four or five shillings a-day; they would be the citizens of a free government, and enjoy all the rights which Englishmen possess;

they would live in a climate as healthy as our own, and they would join nations which speak our language, which inherit our instincts, and which honour our institutions. In fact those who live here in poverty without the slightest hope of advancement might feel when they had emigrated, that a career of affluence, and an honourable social position was open both to them and their children. But we must remember that there are many obstacles which prevent labour passing from one country to another, with the same rapidity with which capital is transferred from one investment to another, when the realization of larger profits appears to be probable. There are powerful feelings, which are implanted by nature in the human breast; thus, love of country is an instinct which has preserved society, and which has prompted man to perform some of his noblest deeds. Again, the human character would soon be corrupted by selfishness and by other evil passions, if men did not feel a strong affection for their family, for their friends, and for their early associations. We may therefore hope that men will always show a great reluctance to leave their native land, and consequently some very powerful motive must operate to induce people to emigrate.

But love of country and affection for family and friends have not been the only causes which

have restrained the English and Scotch from emi-
grating. It is well known that the more ignorant
people are, the more terrified they feel at the
prospect of a long sea-voyage.

Unskilled workmen, such as agricultural labourers, are those who obtain the greatest benefit
from emigration. In the first place, these are the
labourers who in our own country are the worst
paid, and these labourers moreover supply that
kind of labour which is most required in young
countries. When a nation accumulates wealth, a
demand arises for commodities, which only can be
made by workmen who possess refined taste and
delicate skill. The peculiar qualities which give
value to the labour of our more skilled artisans
would be of little use to the emigrant, for he has
often to be the pioneer of civilization in the
boundless prairies of the far West, or in the almost
untrodden wilds of Australia. He therefore needs
a strong constitution, a muscular frame, and that
determined energy which arises from physical
strength. Agriculture is almost certain to be the
chief industry of a young colony; manufactures
cannot thrive until population so increases that
large masses of people are aggregated together.
Consequently agricultural labourers, and others
who are accustomed to outdoor employment have
been chiefly those who have emigrated from our

country; but it so happens that these individuals are amongst the most ignorant of our population; our emigrants have been drawn from a class who would be most powerfully affected by a dread of the dangers and difficulties to be encountered in distant lands. From these and various other reasons, emigration from England and Scotland has not yet been on a sufficiently large scale to cause a serious disturbance in any branch of industry. It may in fact be said, that hitherto this emigration has produced unmixed good. Our surplus population has alone been drafted off, and no branch of industry has as yet been impeded by a deficiency in the supply of labour. If this surplus population had not been thus absorbed, labour would no doubt be cheaper, but I doubt if this would have conferred any real benefit upon the capitalist class, for it must be remembered that when men are unemployed they become a useless and a very expensive burden; they have to be maintained by parish relief, and each advance in the poor-rates really takes so much from the profits realised upon the capital invested in business. For instance, it is quite certain, that during the last few years, emigration has produced a very considerable advance in the wages of all our labourers; and yet I believe that the average rate of profit obtained by employers has increased, instead of being reduced. It is a well-established principle in Political Economy, that the rate of profit depends upon the cost of labour, and that the cost of labour is determined, not only by the wages paid, but also by the amount of work which is really done for these wages. Many of our labourers at the present time can barely obtain a sufficiency of the necessaries of life. A reduction in their wages might diminish their strength, and in this way the cost of labour might be increased instead of being lessened. We can all appreciate the false economy which would be practised, if a horse was so much stinted of food, that he could only do half as much work as he would be able to perform if he was properly fed.

These considerations justify the conclusion that emigration has achieved the great result of benefiting those who have left our shores, and at the same time has effected a marked improvement in the condition of our home population; moreover, these striking advantages have been secured, without causing the slightest loss to the rest of the community. There are however other most important consequences which have resulted from emigration. I have already told you that as a nation advances in population and wealth, food has a tendency to become more expensive. Hence arises the chief economic difficulty which a pro-

sperous nation, such as England, has to surmount.
For it is manifest that if food becomes more expensive, wages must be advanced in order to prevent a deterioration in the condition of the labourer.
But the profits of the capitalist must be diminished, if wages are advanced in order to compensate
the labourer for an increase in the cost of living.
The amount of capital which is accumulated, depends *cæteris paribus* upon the average rate of profit
which can be realised. Hence dear food is prejudi-
cial both to employers and employed. The employer suffers, because he is obliged to pay higher
wages, and the employed cannot continue to obtain such additional wages as will recompense
him for a rise in the price of food; since if profits
are diminished less capital will be accumulated,
and therefore a less aggregate amount will be
distributed in wages. It consequently becomes of
great importance both to employers and employed
that the cost of the ordinary necessaries of life
should not be augmented.

The cheap food which is thus so essential to us
as a nation, is to a great extent supplied to us from
those countries whose resources have been chiefly
developed by our emigrants. Our average importation of wheat is not less than five million quar-
ters; a very considerable portion of this is sent
to us from the Western States of America, where

boundless tracts of the richest corn-land in the
world still remain uncultivated; each emigrant
who tills this productive soil increases the quantity
of cheap food which can be imported into our own
country. Emigration consequently not only im-
proves the condition of our people by drawing off
our surplus population, but it also confers a signal
benefit both upon the labourer and upon his
master; for through its agency a bountiful supply
of cheap food is afforded, and if this cheap food
was not forthcoming, an increasing population
must gradually decline in prosperity.

But may not emigration proceed too far? This
is a question which may be most reasonably asked,
and it is one which well deserves to be most
carefully considered. I have already remarked,
that emigration, when once begun, continues for
some time to operate with increasing force. No
one, for instance, can think that the agricultural
labourer can have any valid reason to remain
here, working hard for nine or ten shillings a week,
when either in America or in our colonies, employers would most gladly give him four or five
times as much for his labour. But the agricultural
labourer is so stationary, because his energy has
been damped by ignorance, and all enterprise has
been destroyed in him by the dull routine in which
he has passed his life. Each man who emigrates

and achieves success, is certain to cause his example to be followed by many of his former friends
and associates. They will receive from him a glow-
ing picture of his new life. He will entreat them
to come and forsake their poverty for the affluence which he is now enjoying, and they will
learn from him that it is easy to surmount the
many difficulties and dangers with which a voyage
to a foreign country has been associated in their
minds. The tide of emigration continues to flow
with such startling rapidity from Ireland, chiefly
because those who have already emigrated are not
only constantly encouraging others to follow their
example, but are also supplying them with the
money to pay for their passage and outfit. It
therefore seems to be by no means improbable
that in the course of a few years there may be a
much greater emigration from our agricultural
districts than has ever been known before. Already
an alarm is occasionally heard from some of our
farmers, that there is a scarcity of labour. Up to
the present time, emigration has not produced such
an effect upon wages as might have been anticipated, and the reason of this is, that we had a
surplus population which could be drawn upon for
a considerable period without producing much
effect upon wages. Let it, however now, not be
forgotten, that this source of supply is exhausted,

for at the present time it may be said, that all
our able-bodied labourers who are anxious to work
can find employment. We have been so long
accustomed to speak of our increasing population,
that it becomes difficult for us to grapple with the
significant fact, that the population of the United
Kingdom is at the present time stationary. The
last returns of the Registrar General prove that
emigration is at the present time so great, that
it almost exactly absorbs the excess of births
over deaths. This statistical fact implies so many
considerations of such vital importance that it may
be considered to denote a new epoch in the economic history of this country.

Our population during each successive period
of our history has been steadily augmenting. Frequently, population advanced more rapidly than
capital was accumulated, and this was especially
the case during the earlier years of the present
century. At that time the supply of labour greatly
exceeded the demand. Consequently there was
then a large surplus of unemployed labour. Those
who could not find work were maintained by parochial relief, and hence the poor-rates gradually absorbed an increasing portion of the aggregate
wealth of the country. The burden which was thus
cast upon industry so seriously impeded commercial activity, that the industry of the country might

have been permanently crippled. It therefore became absolutely necessary to impose more stringent conditions upon those able-bodied labourers who sought relief. The desired object was effected by the celebrated Poor Law Act of 1834. The great end sought to be attained by this Act was to limit out-door relief, and since that time every one who claims parochial assistance can be compelled to become an inmate of the Union Workhouse. The able-bodied have always shown a great repugnance to the discipline and the restraints to which they must submit whilst they remain in the poorhouse. Hence since 1834, parochial relief has been seldom sought, except by those who are either helpless or really destitute.

But reverting to those times when labour was redundant, you will readily perceive that the wages of the worst-paid labourers would only just suffice to provide them with a bare subsistence, when there was a dearth of employment for those who were willing to work. When such a state of things existed, no employer would be compelled to pay more than what may be termed 'Pauper wages;' if his labourers were not satisfied to work for such a remuneration, those who were unemployed would be thankful to work for him, if the wages which he offered them would secure them any small advantages or comforts which they were unable to obtain from parochial relief. You will therefore find that the speculations of the eminent Political Economists, such as Ricardo and Malthus, who wrote at the period to which I am alluding, invariably assume as an axiom, that the remuneration of our worst-paid labourers is so small as to keep them constantly on the verge of pauperism. These eminent writers are even now often ignorantly described as if they were too hard-hearted to have any generous sympathies. Malthus and Ricardo, however, devoted their powerful and humane minds to understand the causes which produced, and thence to discover the remedies which would alleviate, the distressing poverty with which their country was afflicted. They appreciated the full force of the truth that the wages of many labourers would continue to represent nothing more than a bare subsistence as long as there was a surplus unemployed population. This conviction induced Malthus to write his celebrated Essay on Population, for the main object of this work was to prove that the condition of mankind must deteriorate unless population was restrained. The opinions which were expressed by Malthus have been frequently misrepresented; for it has been stated that all his conclusions were based upon the principle, that population increases in a geometric ratio, whereas food only increases in an arithmetic ratio. The employment of such language was no doubt unfortunate; yet no one who reads Malthus, with an unprejudiced mind, can fail to be convinced by the truths which he demonstrated. We must all admit that it has been conclusively established by experience, that man's power to multiply his species is so great, that a country would sooner or later be unable to support its population, unless causes were brought into operation which either restrained or diminished it.

Malthus, in his Essay, gave a most detailed and interesting account of the various checks which restrain population in different countries, and in different periods of history. In all countries which are comparatively uncivilized, the increase of population has been chiefly prevented by war, and by those periodic visitations of famine and disease which seem to be the certain companions of barbarism. As nations become civilized, the forces of nature are made more obedient to man's control, and famines become much less frequent. The laws of health are better understood and more studiously regarded, and consequently man is no longer devastated by those plagues which in former ages so often decimated a nation. It might therefore be thought that population, unrestrained by these checks, would, in the most civilized countries, advance with marvellous rapidity. The present cen-

tury has however witnessed no such increase of
population in any European country, and the reason of this it is not difficult to understand.   Utter
recklessness with regard to the future is one of the
surest marks of barbarism.   But as people become
more civilized, their acts are more frequently controlled by prudent foresight; the responsibility of
causing children to be born into the world will not
be incurred, unless parents consider that they possess the requisite means to rear, to educate, and to
maintain, the social position of these children.
These are the feelings which chiefly impede the
full increase of population in such countries as
Great Britain.   It must however be borne in mind,
that these feelings act with very different force
upon different classes in the same country.   People
may become so miserably poor, that they cease to
have any care for the future.   Thus the wretched
cottiers of Ireland married with utter recklessness.
No ray of hope ever penetrated their abject poverty; and whether they had a large family or not,
their only prospect seemed to be to obtain just
sufficient subsistence to keep them on the verge of
starvation; they were hopelessly in debt to their
landlords; and hence any surplus which their industry might yield, was as it were absorbed in this
insatiable gulf.

Our worst paid labourers in England and

Scotland have perhaps never felt their condition to be one of utter hopelessness; and consequently in these countries, an increase of population amongst even the very poor, has always been restrained by some prudential considerations. If the material condition of our labourers should improve, they will gradually become accustomed to recognise as essential to their happiness a standard of living, with which is associated an increasing amount of comfort. Many individuals in the middle and upper classes are often for a time compelled to resist the desire which they may feel to marry, because they are impressed with the conviction, that they cannot afford it. But when a man engaged in a profession or trade says that he cannot afford to marry, what does this mean? He would not starve if he married; but he may perhaps think that he should act wrongly if he brought children into the world, unless he could give them the education, or the comforts, which he has had the advantage of enjoying himself.

I trust you will not think when I make these allusions to the speculations of Malthus, I am anxious to express an opinion, that our own countrymen, by placing restraints upon population, will either augment their own happiness, or increase the general well-being of mankind. I have referred to Malthus, because at the time when he wrote, the truth of the principle was receiving a terrible verification, that the material condition of the people will decline if population is permitted so rapidly to increase, that the surplus of unemployed labour becomes steadily augmented. I know it may be said, and said with truth, that the world is as yet most sparsely peopled; there are still vast tracts as yet scarcely trodden by man, which are gifted with such great natural resources, that they might become the home of mighty, happy, and prosperous nations. A glance at the map of the world will abundantly verify the truth of this fact. Australia, for instance, has been only partly explored, and we make a most moderate computation if we say that a population of 100,000,000 might live there with every comfort that man could require. Again, it has been calculated that the valley of the Mississippi, if it was cultivated with as much care as our own country, would grow enough wheat to feed all the inhabitants now existing on this earth. Without specially alluding to particular localities, a moment's reflection will convince you, that in Europe, Asia, Africa, and America, there are tracts of land now unpeopled, which, if they were properly cultivated, might support a population as numerous and as wealthy as that which exists on the soil of these islands.

The truth therefore becomes irresistibly brought home to our minds, that if a man finds his labour is not wanted in one country, he ought not to stagnate there in hopeless poverty; there is placed before him in other lands a great and glorious career; a great career, because he may become the progenitor of mighty nations; a glorious career, because he will abundantly fulfil the behests of his Maker, if he causes the wilderness to become the home of civilised man. This world was made for the occupation of the human race, and it never could be intended that fertile soils should grow nothing but rank and useless vegetation; it never could be intended, that rivers which might stimulate the production of untold wealth should always continue to flow through solitudes; it never could be intended, we may unhesitatingly say, that scenes should continue to be viewed by no human eye, which are so beautiful, that their contemplation must make man look from Nature up to Nature's God.

The experience of the last century would seem to show, that it is peculiarly the destined mission of our own country to become the mother of nations. Small as is the area of these islands, they have chiefly supplied the emigrants, from whom have sprung the population which now occupies the vast continent of North America. Already there are not less than 30,000,000 on American soil who speak our language, and who must look to us as their progenitors; before 100 years have passed, the number will probably be quadrupled. In the course of a few years, our emigrants have founded the Australian colonies, and already more than a million of British subjects are living there in a state of comfort and affluence, which our own labourers unfortunately do not enjoy. Twenty years since, the colony of Victoria was little more than a vast unoccupied pasture; it now has a great trade, it has a constitutional Parliament, in which State questions are discussed with great ability; and its capital city, Melbourne, has streets and buildings which would do honour to our most thriving towns. These are the facts which give to England her special greatness and her peculiar glory. The mighty nations which have existed in bygone ages have perished, and have left behind them no living testimony. Greece was adorned with a civilisation which has in many respects never been equalled. No prodigies of valour have ever surpassed those which were performed by Grecian heroes. Grecian buildings have had to bear the ravages of time, and yet their exquisite beauty still suggests models for modern architects to strive to imitate. Greek orators, Greek poets, and Greek historians, have left behind them only

fragments of their works, and yet they form the
finest literature which one language ever produced.
Again, Rome had an empire as vast as our own,
and yet when the greatness of Greece and Rome
had departed, they left behind them, as it were, no
offspring to inherit their institutions, and to trans-
mit their glory from generation to generation. Our
countrymen, without feeling any excess of national
pride, may reasonably believe that the greatness
of our race will be perpetuated, although Great Britain may not maintain her present pre-eminence.

But amidst the emotions which reflections on
such topics as these suggest, let us not forget some
of the more immediate consequences which may
result from the tendency which our labourers now
exhibit to emigrate to any locality where their
labour will receive its best reward. Two agencies
of potent influence which scarcely existed in the
days of earlier Political Economists are each year
operating with increasing force. In the first place,
it must have been remarked by all observers, that
until recent times modern nations were in a state
of chronic war. Legislators moreover framed
protective tariffs with the view of impeding commercial intercourse; hence capital was only in a
slight degree transmitted from country to country.
But at the present time the capital which one
nation accumulates is not alone applied to support

its own industry; capital is freely sent to any country, if the rate of profit which can be realised upon it is sufficiently attractive. Again, until a recent period, labourers would seldom leave their own country, and they would even often appear bound by an inexorable destiny to remain in the locality in which they were born. When capital and labour thus remain stationary many economic principles could be enunciated which have now lost their applicability. Then it could be said, with approximate truth, that the rate of wages in each country depended upon the number of its labouring population, compared with the amount of capital which was accumulated in that country. But now this principle has to be modified, for only a portion of the wealth which is, for instance, annually saved in England is retained to assist our own industry; the vast sums of English capital which are annually invested in foreign countries do not immediately produce any augmentation in our own wage fund. Formerly, if the births greatly exceeded the deaths, it could positively be asserted, that there would be an increasing number of labourers competing for employment. Now, however, it may happen, that numbers who are born in this country may never seek employment here, but may be drafted off to far distant labour markets.

These considerations show that the principles of Political Economy have to be stated with constantly widening generality. Formerly, the condition of any class of labourers was mainly determined by the amount of capital accumulated in one district, compared with the number of labourers who happened to be born in that particular locality. In different counties of England, the same kind of labour would receive the most various rates of remuneration. Agricultural labourers might through a long series of years have received fifty per cent. more wages in Yorkshire than in Dorsetshire, and yet no single labourer would leave Dorsetshire, in order to enjoy comparative prosperity in Yorkshire. This immobility of the labourer was partly due to ignorance and to the want of enterprise which ignorance engenders; it was, however, chiefly encouraged by the Laws of Settlement, which were connected with our system of poor-relief. These Laws of Settlement, which may be regarded as amongst the most cruel wrongs that ever oppressed a class, are now happily modified by a more enlightened legislation. Railways and other improvements in the means of communication have wonderfully increased the facility of passing from one locality to another, and education has made the labourers more enterprising. All these influences have combined to cause the remuneration which is paid for the same kind of labour in different parts of the same country, to approximate each year more and more to uniformity. This tendency to equalise the wages which are paid for the same kind of work in different localities of the same country, will gradually extend its influence, and labourers will show a greater willingness to emigrate, if in other countries their labour will receive a higher remuneration.

Let us therefore for a moment reflect upon the position of an agricultural labourer in England, and then let us ascertain what will be his lot if he emigrates to Australia. The average weekly earnings of a Dorsetshire or Wiltshire labourer, do not certainly exceed eleven shillings a week. In the winter months, he only receives nine shillings a week, in the summer, he not unfrequently earns twelve or fifteen shillings a week; but it must be remembered that these wages are obtained for piece-work, and they really indicate not a higher remuneration for labour, but that the workman has an opportunity of making overtime. An English mower or reaper will commence work at four o'clock in the morning, and with two hours' rest for breakfast and dinner, will often continue his monotonous and severe exertion until seven or eight o'clock in the evening. The human frame is probably incapable of greater physical effort.

From these average weekly wages of eleven shillings, one shilling has to be deducted for house-rent, and ten shillings remain to supply the labourer with food and clothing. This amount barely suffices to give him a sufficiency of the necessary and essential comforts of life, even supposing that he is a single man, but if the ordinary English agricultural labourer has a wife and family, it can be readily demonstrated by the simplest calculation that ten shillings a week will not always bring to that household enough food to satisfy hunger*, or sufficient fuel and clothing to provide an adequate protection against the cold of our rigorous climate. As I have before said, many collateral evils result from this poverty; a father is driven, as it were by dire necessity, to send his children to work, directly they can earn the smallest wages. For how can we expect that the claims of education will be considered, when the two shillings a week, which is given to a child for holloaing at crows, or driving a plough, will perhaps alleviate the hunger of a family, or permit a little more fuel to give some additional warmth to a dreary and comfortless cottage. Children are thus taken away from school when they are eight years old, the

---

* The medical officer of the Board of Health has recently declared, after a most careful investigation, that one-fifth of our population have not a sufficiency of food and clothing.

little they have ever been taught is forgotten; the consequence is, that a great proportion of our agricultural population can neither read nor write. It is, moreover, evident that this melancholy ignorance is due to causes, which are neither affected by improved schools, nor by a cheap and extending literature.

In Australia, a first-class agricultural labourer can readily obtain seven shillings a day; these wages are four times as great as those which are paid in England. The cost of living is probably not greater in the one country than in the other; some commodities are comparatively dear in Australia, whereas others are remarkably cheap. All the first necessaries of life, such as bread and meat, are much cheaper there than in England. All articles of Eastern produce, such as tea, coffee, and sugar are cheaper, because they have to be imported from a shorter distance, and the custom duties levied in Australia are much lighter than those that are imposed by our own tariff. Scarcity of labour of course makes all manufactured articles dear in Australia; but such commodities can be imported from England, and there therefore cannot permanently be any greater difference in the price of clothes and other wearing apparel in Australia and in England than would be sufficient to cover the cost of carriage between the one country and the other. It consequently appears that the wages of the ordinary labourer estimated not only in money, but also in the amount of commodities which these wages will purchase, are four times as great in Australia as they are in England. It has been sometimes asserted that the wonderful material prosperity which is conferred by emigration upon the English labourer is more apparent than real; such opinions however are not always disinterested. Australia has a climate as healthy as our own. A settler in that country does not seek a home amongst those who are strangers to his race and language; the Australians are socially an integral part of the British Empire; our Queen has not more loyal subjects; they speak our language; they read our literature, their tastes and their pursuits are the same as our own, and they pursue with eagerness the sports and amusements, which have done so much to mould our national character. If a traveller walks along the streets of Melbourne, he would not know but that he was in an English city possessing a peculiar beauty and magnificence; its situation is picturesque, its inhabitants are wealthy, and its streets obtain from their width an architectural beauty, which is unknown in those countries where towns have not been built and arranged, until land possessed a monopoly value.

An English labourer moreover has no definite prospect of improving his lot; his life is a severe struggle for existence; those who are born to work for daily wages end their days in the same position; an agricultural labourer would be obliged to make severe sacrifices to save £200, and if he succeeded in this difficult achievement, our poor law system would prevent his position being in the least degree superior to the position of one who never attempted to save a shilling. The guardians who administer the poor-rates, would immediately say to the man who had saved, You possess so many shillings a week, and therefore we shall deduct this amount from the relief which we grant you, if you apply to us for assistance, either in old age or sickness. Contrast the melancholy hopelessness of such a career, with the future which is placed before every man who is willing to be industrious, where labour is remunerated as highly as it is in Australia. The facts which have been adduced, prove that the Australian settler who earns his six or seven shillings a day might with ordinary prudence annually save £50, and the eligible investments which are offered to him for his capital are such as can never be enjoyed in an old country. It is a well-established principle in economic science, that where fertile land is abundant and consequently cheap, a high rate of profit will inevitably prevail; on the other hand, the rate of profit will be low, where the resources of the land must, as it were, be severely strained, in order to provide food for an increasing population. England and Australia illustrate the truth of this principle. In the former country, a good security such as a freehold mortgage, will not yield more than 4½ per cent. interest, whereas in Australia the interest which can be obtained for a similar investment is not less than 8 per cent. Again the desire to acquire land, a taste which seems to be implanted in us all by nature, can rarely be gratified by our own labourers. The ownership of landed property is each year more and more becoming a luxury which none but the very wealthy can hope to enjoy. Our law favours the aggregation of land into large properties, and with the growth of national wealth, a greater number compete for the limited quantity of land which is brought into the market. In Australia however, the whole community may become landed proprietors; three or four years of thrift will make the Australian labourer the owner of the land which he cultivates.

The emigrant moreover loses nothing with regard to political privileges; we speak with just and natural pride of a constitution which gives us all equality under the law, and which secures

us the broadest freedom, both in thought and
speech. But our legislators have up to the present time supposed that the working classes cannot with safety and advantage be permitted to
take part in the government of the country. They
have to bear the burden of severe taxation without enjoying Parliamentary representation; their
welfare is materially affected by laws in the enact-
ment of which they have no voice; wars are declared, and they have no representatives to give
effect to the opinions which they may hold upon
the policy which leads to hostilities; yet the war
may cause thousands of lives to be sacrificed, may
cause millions of treasure to be squandered, and
may thus bring death and sorrow to many a humble home, and may place a more onerous burden
of taxation upon unborn generations of those who
have to work for daily wages. I do not wish here
to express political sentiments. This is not the
place either to enlarge upon the dangers, or to
speak of the advantages of an extended suffrage.
I am simply endeavouring to describe the salient
points of difference in the condition of the emigrant and of the home labourer, and this comparison would be incomplete, if I did not allude
to the fact, that in our own country, the working
man seldom possesses the franchise, when at the
same time our colonial constitutions give the suf-

frage to every adult who is not disqualified by the commission of some crime.

In my opinion, the facts which have been here adduced render it impossible for us to resist the conclusion, that at the present time, emigration would effect a most decided improvement in the material condition of the great mass of our ordinary labourers. When moreover it has been shown that the emigrant has to submit to no social or political disadvantages, I think that to every one who takes an interest in the future of this country, there is a subject suggested for the most anxious and serious reflection. For if our labouring population would gain by leaving their own country, can we feel any real security that we shall be able to retain a sufficient amount of labour to support our present industrial development. Ireland still has to witness that exodus of her population, which has now continued with steady force for so many years; and we cannot expect, nor ought we to desire, that labourers will remain in England to drag out a miserable existence on nine or ten shillings a week*. I would earnestly entreat our commercial men to think upon this subject before it

* At the present time (the autumn of 1865), the emigration from the port of Liverpool alone, is at the rate of 160,000 a year. Although trade has revived, the present emigration shows an increase of 30 per cent. over the emigration of last year.

is too late. I venture to ask them no longer to estimate the prosperity of the country by the amount of wealth which is produced. Let them inquire how that wealth is distributed, for, we may depend upon it, that the welfare of the country is not increased, but, that on the contrary, its greatness is being rapidly undermined, if those who possess vast wealth become still more wealthy, whilst at the same time, the poverty of the poor receives no alleviation. Our leading statesmen have been too prone to measure the weal of the country by a fallacious statistical standard. Around us, on every side, there are striking evidences of wealth being accumulated with unexampled rapidity. Our exports and imports have in a few years trebled. The soil is better cultivated, all the material resources of the country are developed with the greatest skill and enterprise, and there are all the outward tokens of vast wealth. When we observe these things we are inclined to say, Mark, what proofs of national prosperity! But let it be remembered, that the labourers may observe the same facts, and then let me ask, if some very different thoughts will not be suggested to their minds.

A man may perhaps have worked upon the same farm all his life; he may remember how its cultivation has improved, and how the produce raised from it has been increased, yet he finds that he is still living in the same miserable two-roomed hovel; his children herd together in the same way that children herded together when he was young; he is ignorant, and so are his children; his father came upon the parish when his work was done; he can anticipate no other ending to his own life, for he has not been able to save a single shilling. The working miner hears that those for whom he is labouring have accumulated gigantic fortunes, and yet he finds that as he advances scarcely beyond the prime of life, his industrial career is virtually ended; for with a constitution ruined by the unhealthiness of his employment, he has to face the miseries of poverty. Those labourers who have been the constructors of our docks, our railways, and our canals; works which have yielded untold wealth, too often find that while these mighty industrial improvements have been achieved, they who make them, have to live in dwellings where no comfort can be enjoyed, and where every decency of life has to be forgotten. Let us not forget, that whilst we are congratulating ourselves upon our national prosperity, thoughts such as those I have just described may stimulate great masses of our population to seek those countries, where they believe that labour will receive a higher reward, and a more satisfactory recognition. I therefore feel

that it is of urgent importance that our labourers
should become more wealthy, and their condition
more satisfactory; for if these ends cannot be attained, we shall lose, through emigration, the élite
of our labouring population; the intelligent and
enterprising will go forth first, and leave this country burdened with the young, the old, and the
indolent.

It may perhaps be thought, that I, in express-
ing these opinions, am forgetting the strict principles of economic science, and that I am permitting
myself to be influenced by the sentimentality of a
vague philanthropy. I feel confident however, that
I shall be able to convince you, that I advocate no
remedial measures which are opposed to any single
principle of economic science. I will therefore
commence, by recalling to your mind the simple
laws which regulate wages. You will remember
that the average rate of wages which prevails in
any country depends upon a ratio between capital
and population, and the wages which are paid in
any particular industry depend upon the amount
of capital invested in that industry, compared with
the number of labourers, who seek to be employed
in that special branch of business. At the present
time in this country there are not too many labourers; no ablebodied man has a difficulty in
obtaining employment; the prosperity of the coun-

try will therefore be impaired if an advance in wages should be obtained through a decline in the number of our labouring population; for unless there is a surplus population, the labourers cannot decrease in number without affecting our industry, and without also depriving us of one of the elements of our national greatness; since we conceive that the greatness of a country is to be tested by increasing happiness diffused amongst a larger population.

As therefore we do not wish to see our population decrease, and as wages can only be advanced, either by an increase of capital, or by a decrease in the number of labourers, we are reduced to a consideration of the following problem, What can be done to cause more capital to be distributed in wages? It will be at once admitted that the amount of capital invested in any industry, is determined by the rate of profit; the greater is the rate of profit, the greater will be the amount of capital embarked. It might therefore appear that we are placed in a hopeless dilemma; for if wages are advanced, the expenses of production are augmented; the profits of the employer will consequently be decreased, and he will be induced to invest less capital in his industry. Hence it appears that no advance in wages can permanently be maintained, which tends to diminish the rate of profit.

16

It may however perhaps be thought, that employers could charge a higher price for the commodities which they produce, and thus compensate themselves for the payment of additional
wages. I have already alluded to various agencies which may be brought into operation, and
which may prejudicially affect both employers
and employed, if an additional remuneration to
labour causes the price of commodities to be increased. Thus, suppose the wages of English
operatives were so much increased that English
manufacturers could not obtain an adequate rate
of profit, unless they raised the price of their
goods 10 per cent. If England was commercially isolated from the rest of the world, this
augmentation in price might be fairly regarded
as beneficial, because it was due to a circumstance which would denote a more satisfactory
distribution of wealth; those who purchased manufactured goods would of course have to pay
more for them; but this could not be regretted,
since labour would be better remunerated. But
England is not commercially isolated; both her
import and her export trade extend over the
world; in many branches of industry, there is between her and other countries a keenly contested
competition. If the foreign producers could obtain any relative advantage, our own manufac-

turers would be undersold, both in the home and
foreign market, and the existence of important
trades would be imperilled. This consequently is
a danger, which may threaten our commercial prosperity, if emigration from these shores should continue, and should thus so diminish the supply of
labour, as to cause wages to advance, and thus
make the cost of labour here to be greater than in
other countries.

Let us therefore inquire whether the danger to
which I have alluded can be averted. It is a danger which not only threatens, but may be regarded
as impending; for nothing seems to be more certain, than that emigration will continue, unless our
labourers become more wealthy and comfortable,
and thus are able to enjoy many of those advantages which now attract them to other lands. Once
more I will venture to impress upon you the fundamental principle, that the condition of the labourer cannot be permanently improved, if the additional remuneration which he receives diminishes
the profits of the employers. But can no change
be effected in our present industrial economy?
Can no arrangements be adopted which will cause
labour to be more efficient in the production of
wealth? If the same amount of labour produced
an increased quantity of wealth, there would then
be more to be distributed both amongst the em-

ployers and the employed, and profits and wages might both be augmented.

It appears to me that the reply which can be given to these questions will determine what will be the industrial future of this country. In attempting to supply an answer, I wish you to remember that in this country, industry is carried on by capitalists and by labourers; these two classes consider that they have distinct interests, and between them there is consequently no bond of pecuniary sympathy. I believe it is only by modifying these unsatisfactory industrial relations that we can hope to retain the best portion of our industrial population; for it should not be forgotten, that at the present time many countries are eagerly competing for the skill and the energy of the British labourer.

I am chiefly induced to anticipate the future of our country with confidence and with hope, because each year supplies some gratifying indication, that our present industrial economy is susceptible of a beneficent change. Twenty years since cooperation was looked upon as the mischievous dream of democrats, and copartnership was never mentioned, without provoking the contemptuous derision of practical men. You are familiar with some of the great achievements of the cooperative movement; and before many years have passed, there is every reason to suppose that in many of our largest commercial establishments, a copartnership between capital and labour will have been established. It is impossible to exaggerate the blessings and the material advantages which may result from thus uniting capital and labour, for the antagonism of these interests has been fruitful of the most baneful consequences.

Some successful schemes of copartnership have been described in a previous chapter. The Messrs. Crossley of Halifax, who employ between 4000 and 5000 hands, and whose carpet manufactory is perhaps the largest in the world, have established a copartnership between capital and labour. They have converted their business into a joint-stock company; they have retained a certain proportion of the shares themselves, and have preferentially allotted the remainder amongst their workmen. The workmen are to be represented on the board of direction. It is manifest that those who are employed in this establishment are placed in an entirely different position compared with the ordinary labourers. The antagonism of interests between employers and employed is at once destroyed, and thus harmony and sympathy will take the place of hostility and distrust. The dull monotony which must depress human energy if no other prospect is offered except to work through life for daily wages will rapidly vanish; for a man's career will seem to be bright with hope and promise, if he knows that some self-denial will enable him to save sufficient to make him a partner in the particular business to which his labour is applied.

It will of course be said that such schemes are impracticable, that trade could not be carried on, if masters were subject to the interference which they would have to endure, supposing they permitted their labourers to become, even in a modified sense, their partners. But the practical difficulties of the scheme will soon receive a solution. It need only be said that those who have suggested and are making the experiment, are men who are unrivalled for their commercial sagacity and ability; they speak confidently of its success. The ground of this confident hope can be briefly and simply stated. The labourer's position will be vastly improved by copartnership, and therefore his labour will become much more efficient. Under our present industrial system, there is no force constantly in operation, to call forth the utmost energy and skill of the industrial classes. The remuneration of labour is regarded as a transaction of buying and selling; labourers are therefore frequently tempted to do as little work as possible for the wages received. Hence

although a very great expense may be incurred
by employing foremen and others to overlook
labourers, yet no amount of watching can be so
effectual as to prevent work being often shirked
and badly done. These defects which so seriously
diminish the efficiency of labour would evidently
be cured by copartnership; if therefore this new
industrial system can be successfully introduced,
the great economic problem of the age will have
been solved. The labourer will have been made
more wealthy, more happy, and more comfortable,
and at the same time the prosperity of other
classes will be in no degree diminished; because
if labour is made more efficient, there will be a
greater amount of wealth to distribute amongst all
classes of society.

I moreover believe that as the labourers gradually become both morally and materially improved by copartnership, they will be trained to
enjoy a higher phase of social life; for although
we may be sincere admirers of the cooperative
movement, yet we cannot fairly conceal from ourselves the fact, that the past life of the labourers
of this country has not fitted the bulk of them
immediately to partake of the advantages of cooperation. They must receive some preliminary
training; they must be taught some economic
truths, and copartnership is admirably fitted to

give this training, and supply this teaching.   Thus the workmen who become partners in the Messrs. Crossley's establishment, will have impressed upon them by the force of experience, some of the most important truths in economic science.   They will themselves witness the functions which capital performs, and they will consequently soon cease to rail against capital as if it exercised a despotic power over them.   They will also become acquainted with the requisites for commercial success, and they will soon perceive that no mercantile skill can always avert depression in trade. They will also quickly discover that periods of great prosperity are often succeeded by periods of corresponding adversity; they will therefore know that the most thriving establishment would soon be ruined, if there was not sufficient prudence on the part of the managers, to set aside a portion of the great gains which are realised when trade is good, and thus create a reserve fund, which will enable trade to be continued when either only inadequate profits can be realised, or when perhaps heavy losses have to be incurred.   As this varied experience is brought to bear upon the labourer, his whole character will receive such salutary training, as to fit him to participate in all the advantages of cooperation.

But as we dwell upon this possible future, so

bright and so happy for the working classes, and so encouraging to every one who is anxious for the welfare of his fellow-man, an interesting reflection may be suggested. Although in distant parts of the world, great, wealthy, and populous nations have been founded by European emigrants, yet hitherto there has been no immigration of labour into Europe from other countries which may be more thickly peopled, and in which labour receives a lower remuneration. Neither have labourers emigrated to any great extent from one European country to another, although in most of these countries very different rates of wages prevail. Wages are lower in Germany than in England, yet Germans have not emigrated to this country in sufficient numbers to produce any perceptible effect; they have however thronged in such multitudes to the United States, that the traveller in the far West may often imagine, as he passes through one of the many towns which have there sprung up with such startling rapidity, that he is in Germany; the people are German, the language he hears spoken is German, and they still retain many of the tastes and manners which they had in their own fatherland. When these facts are before us, can it be regarded as an impossible contingency, that in the course of a few years there may be a migration of labour on a large scale from one European country to another?

The condition of our own labourers must rapidly improve, when emigration becomes, as it has become in Ireland, a great national movement. If therefore emigration continues, the labourers who remain here will gradually find that their industry will obtain as high a remuneration as it would obtain, either in the Colonies, or in the United States. But since our own country may before long possess almost the same economic advantages for the labourer as the United States or the Colonies, what is there to prevent the tide of European emigration flowing to us? A long, expensive, and a wearisome voyage would be saved; moreover, it must be borne in mind that all the tendencies of the present age, encourage such a migration between contiguous countries. If we place faith in the progress of civilization, we must believe that war will become less frequent, and that the barriers of prejudice and antipathy which have separated nation from nation, will be gradually swept away. It was formerly thought that hatred of foreigners exhibited all the virtues of high-minded patriotism. But the time is rapidly coming, when those most distinguished for virtue and nobility of character must have a wider sympathy than love of country. A desire

to see your own countrymen prosperous and happy
will then be regarded as selfish and narrow-minded,
if it is not associated with a sincere anxiety for
the welfare of the whole human race. As the
prejudice against foreign countries declines, an
increasing readiness will be shown to pass from
one country to another, in order to secure a higher
remuneration for labour. Agencies will in fact
be brought into operation, similar to those which
at the present time cause capital to be readily
transferred from one country to another. In those
days when wars were constant, and a general
distrust was thus engendered, almost the whole
of the capital which England accumulated was
invested in her own industry. Now however English savings are distributed over the world; let it
only be proved that an industrial enterprise is
likely to be profitable, and English capital is
sure to be forthcoming.

But there is another migration of labour which
is perhaps destined to be far more momentous
in its consequences than the one to which we
have been referring; for to what an extent may
not the future of the human race be affected, if
the densely populated, and comparatively uncivilized East should pour vast crowds of labourers
into the civilized countries of the Western world?
China has a population of more than 300,000,000,

and her numbers are only kept within these limits by an actual want of subsistence. If she yielded all the food which might be produced by the proper development of her resources, the population of China would probably be rapidly doubled. Everything connected with this country is strange and anomalous. When Britain was a dreary waste, occupied only by rude savages, China had a peculiar civilization of her own, and had made discoveries in science and art which for centuries were unknown to the Western world. But what China was 2000 years ago, that she is now. She has remained isolated and stationary. The Chinese, confident in their superiority to the rest of mankind, thought that their country would be contaminated, if foreigners were permitted to enter its sacred precincts. But these barriers could not withstand the active commercial enterprise of our country; having once obtained a footing there, we quickly forced our way by fire and by sword, and we have by successive treaties extorted from this inferior race, the right to trade and travel unmolested. But the opening of China may be accompanied with consequences which were probably never anticipated by our statesmen or our merchants. As soon as we forced our way into China, the Chinese seemed ready to meet us with reprisals; they acted as if they wished to say,

You were determined to come to enjoy the advantages which our country could offer to you, and now we will go forth and see, if there are not some benefits which we might obtain in distant lands.

People who are comparatively uncivilized have always shown that there is no wealth which they value so much as the precious metals, and the same feeling which caused such a rush of European and American emigrants to Australia and California, induced vast numbers of Chinese to seek wealth in these newly discovered gold fields. The inhabitants of Australia and California became greatly alarmed. They said, we shall soon be overrun with these yellow-skinned emigrants; all other races will be outnumbered, and our country will be converted into a vast Chinese settlement. Californian politicians were not restrained by checks from a home government; they therefore at once adopted energetic measures, and immediately passed a law which absolutely forbade the Chinese entering the country. The Australian legislatures did not resort to so extreme a remedy. Moreover in these Colonies, there was a great and influential party, whose self-interests prompted them to favour this Chinese immigration. Australia had always wanted labour, and this want was pressing with peculiar intensity, because the gold-fields offered an attraction, which the working classes could not resist. Consequently the advent of these Chinese immigrants solved the difficulty with which the Australian employers had to contend; for it was soon found that the Chinese were cheap and excellent labourers; they were industrious and ingenious, and they proved themselves to be excellent shepherds and gardeners. Hence this Chinese immigration soon became a great question between capital and labour, and the dispute was keenly contested in the Australian Parliaments, and on every hustings. On the one hand the employers urged, that the industry of the country would be paralysed, if labour could not be obtained; and on the other hand, it was vehemently argued that the vices of the Chinese, who were accompanied by no women, would demoralise the community: it was also no doubt perceived, although not so prominently stated, that the remuneration of the wage-receiving class would be seriously diminished, if some check was not imposed upon this inexhaustible supply of labour. The dispute was ultimately settled by a compromise, and a poll-tax of £10 was imposed on all the Chinese who landed on the Australian shores.

This policy must suggest many curious reflections, when we remember how long, how severe, and
how costly has been our struggle to break down
the barriers, which so completely isolated China
from the rest of the world. Moreover we should
ask ourselves, What will England do, and what
would be the effect on our country, if the Chinese
at some future day should show the same anxiety
to come to us, as they have shown to settle in
Australia and California? The contingency may
be thought too improbable and too remote to be
worthy of consideration, yet such speculations may
possess interest and importance, if we desire to
reflect upon the aspect which progressive civilization may in future ages assume. Probably, in
every community, there must be always " hewers
of wood and drawers of water;" and if a whole
nation like our own should advance as greatly in
wealth, intelligence, and happiness, as we could
desire, an inferior race may perhaps come amongst
us, to perform the comparatively menial duties
which industry requires. Increasing enlightenment
and humanity would prevent such a race being
treated with injustice, indignity or cruelty ; liberty
and all the rights of property would be secured
to them, and thus the lot of the whole human
race might be improved, if inferior races were

gradually enlightened and elevated, by bringing them into contact with the ideas and institutions of a high civilization.

FINIS.

CAMBRIDGE: PRINTED AT THE UNIVERSITY PRESS.

16, BEDFORD STREET, COVENT GARDEN, LONDON.
AND AT CAMBRIDGE.

MACMILLAN AND CO.'S
LIST OF PUBLICATIONS.

A BOOK OF THOUGHTS.
By H. A. 18mo. cloth extra, gilt, 3s. 6d.

ACROSS THE CARPA-THIANS. In 1858-60. With a Map. Crown 8vo. 7s. 6d.

ÆSCHYLI EUMENIDES. The Greek Text with English Notes, and an Introduction. By BERNARD DRAKE, M.A. 8vo. 7s. 6d.

AIRY.—TREATISE on the ALGEBRAICAL and NUMERICAL THEORY of ERRORS of OBSERVATIONS, and the Combination of Observations. By G. B. AIRY, M.A. Crown 8vo. 6s. 6d.

ALLINGHAM.— LAURENCE BLOOMFIELD in IRELAND. A Modern Poem. By WILLIAM ALLINGHAM. Fcap. 8vo. 7s.

ANDERSON. — SEVEN MONTHS' RESIDENCE in RUSSIAN POLAND in 1863. By the Rev. FORTESCUE L. M. ANDERSON. Cr. 8vo. 6s.

ANOTHER "STORY of the GUNS;" or Sir Emerson Tennent and the Whitworth Gun. By the "FRASER REVIEWER." Extra fcap. 8vo. 2s.

ANSTED.—THE GREAT STONE BOOK of NATURE. By DAVID THOS. ANSTED, M.A. F.R.S. F.G.S. Fcap. 8vo. 5s.

ANSTIE. — STIMULANTS and NARCOTICS, their MUTUAL RELATIONS. With Special Researches on the Action of Alcohol, Æther, and Chloroform, on the Vital Organism. By FRANCIS E. ANSTIE, M.D. M.R.C.P. 8vo. 14s.

ARISTOTLE ON THE VITAL PRINCIPLE. Translated, with Notes, by CHARLES COLLIER, M.D. F.R.S. Cr. 8vo. 8s. 6d.

ARNOLD. — A FRENCH ETON; or, Middle Class Education and the State. By MATTHEW ARNOLD. Fcap. 8vo. 2s. 6d.

ARNOLD. — ESSAYS on CRITICISM. By MATTHEW ARNOLD, Professor of Poetry in the University of Oxford. Fcp. 8vo. cloth, 6s.

ARTIST and CRAFTSMAN. A Novel. Crown 8vo. 6s.

BAMPTON LECTURES.— *See* BERNARD.

A

BARWELL.—GUIDE in the SICK ROOM. By RICHARD BARWELL, F.R.C.S. Extra fcap. 8vo. 3s. 6d.

BEASLEY.—An ELEMENTARY TREATISE on PLANE TRIGONOMETRY. With a Numerous Collection of Examples. By R. D. BEASLEY, M.A. Crown 8vo. 3s. 6d.

BERNARD. — THE PROGRESS OF DOCTRINE IN THE NEW TESTAMENT. By THOMAS DEHANY BERNARD, M.A. 8vo. cloth, 8s. 6d.

BIRKS.—The DIFFICULTIES of BELIEF in connexion with the CREATION and the FALL. By THOS. RAWSON BIRKS, M.A. Cr. 8vo. 4s. 6d.

BIRKS.—On MATTER and ETHER; or the Secret Laws of Physical Change. By THOS. RAWSON BIRKS, M.A. Cr. 8vo. 5s. 6d.

BLAKE.—THE LIFE OF WILLIAM BLAKE, the Artist. By ALEXR. GILCHRIST. With numerous Illustrations from Blake's Designs and Fac-similes of his Studies of the "Book of Job." 2 vols. Medium 8vo. 32s.

BLANCHE LISLE, AND OTHER POEMS. By CECIL HOME. Fcap. 8vo. 4s. 6d.

BOOLE.—A TREATISE on DIFFERENTIAL EQUATIONS. By GEO. BOOLE, D.C.L. *A New Edition*, revised by I. TODHUNTER, M.A., F.R.S. Crown 8vo. cloth, 14s.

BOOLE.—A TREATISE on the CALCULUS of FINITE DIFFERENCES. By GEO. BOOLE, D.C.L. Crown 8vo. 10s. 6d.

BRIMLEY.—ESSAYS, by the late GEORGE BRIMLEY, M.A. Edited by W. G. CLARK, M.A. With Portrait. *Second Edition.* Fcap. 8vo. 5s.

BROCK.—DAILY READINGS on the PASSION of OUR LORD. By Mrs. H. F. BROCK. Fcap. 8vo. 4s.

BROOK SMITH.—ARITHMETIC in THEORY and PRACTICE. For Advanced Pupils. Part First. By J. BROOK SMITH, M.A. Crown 8vo. 3s. 6d.

BULLOCK—POLISH EXPERIENCES during the INSURRECTION of 1863-4. By W. H. BULLOCK. Crown 8vo. with Map, 8s. 6d.

BURGON.—A TREATISE on the PASTORAL OFFICE. Addressed chiefly to Candidates for Holy Orders, or to those who have recently undertaken the cure of souls. By the Rev. JOHN W. BURGON, M.A. 8vo. 12s.

BUTLER (ARCHER). — WORKS by the Rev. WILLIAM ARCHER BUTLER, M.A. late Professor of Moral Philosophy in the University of Dublin :—

1. SERMONS, DOCTRINAL and PRACTICAL. Edited, with a Memoir of the Author's Life, by THOMAS WOODWARD, M.A. With Portrait. *Sixth Edition.* 8vo. 12s.

2. A SECOND SERIES OF SERMONS. Edited by J. A. JEREMIE, D.D. *Third Edition.* 8vo. 10s. 6d.

3. HISTORY OF ANCIENT PHILOSOPHY. Edited by WM. H. THOMPSON, M.A. 2 vols. 8vo. 1l. 5s.

4. LETTERS ON ROMANISM, in REPLY to MR. NEWMAN'S ESSAY on DEVELOPMENT. Edited by the Very Rev. T. WOODWARD. *Second Edition*, revised by Archdeacon HARDWICK. 8vo. 10s. 6d.

BUTLER (MONTAGU).— SERMONS PREACHED in the CHAPEL of HARROW SCHOOL. By H. MONTAGU BUTLER, Head Master. Crown 8vo. 7s. 6d.

BUTLER. — FAMILY PRAYERS. By the Rev. GEO. BUTLER. Cr. 8vo. 5s.

BUTLER. — SERMONS PREACHED in CHELTENHAM COLLEGE CHAPEL. By the Rev. GEO. BUTLER. Crown 8vo. 7s. 6d.

CAIRNES.—THE SLAVE POWER; its Character, Career, and Probable Designs. Being an Attempt to Explain the Real Issues Involved in the American Contest. By J. E. CAIRNES, M.A. *Second Edition.* 8vo. 10s. 6d.

CALDERWOOD.—PHILOSOPHY of the INFINITE. A Treatise on Man's Knowledge of the Infinite Being, in answer to Sir W. Hamilton and Dr. Mansel. By the Rev. HENRY CALDERWOOD, M.A. *Second Edition.* 8vo. 14s

CAMBRIDGE SENATE-HOUSE PROBLEMS and RIDERS, with SOLUTIONS:—
1848—1851.—By FERRERS and JACKSON. 15s. 6d.
1848—1851. — By JAMESON. 7s. 6d.
1854.—By WALTON and MACKENZIE, M.A. 10s. 6d.
1857.—By CAMPION and WALTON. 8s. 6d.
1860.—ByWATSON and ROUTH. 7s. 6d.
1864.—By WALTON and WILKINSON. 8vo. 10s. 6d.

CAMBRIDGE LENT SERMONS.—SERMONS Preached during LENT, 1864, in Great St. Mary's Church, Cambridge. By the LORD BISHOP OF OXFORD, Rev. H. P. LIDDON, T. L. CLAUGHTON, J. R. WOODFORD, DR. GOULBURN, J. W. BURGON, T. T. CARTER, DR. PUSEY, DEAN HOOK, W. J. BUTLER, DEAN GOODWIN. Crown 8vo. 7s. 6d.

CAMBRIDGE COURSE of ELEMENTARY NATURAL PHILOSOPHY, for the Degree of B.A. Originally compiled by J. C. SNOWBALL, M.A. Late Fellow of St. John's College. *Fifth Edition*, revised and enlarged, and adapted for the Middle Class Examinations by THOMAS LUND, B.D. Crown 8vo. 5s.

CAMBRIDGE. — CAMBRIDGE SCRAP BOOK : containing in a Pictorial Form a Report on the Manners, Customs, Humours, and Pastimes of the University of Cambridge. With nearly 300 Illustrations. *Second Edition.* Crown 4to. 7s. 6d.

A 2

CAMBRIDGE. — CAM-
BRIDGE and DUBLIN MA-
THEMATICAL JOURNAL.
The Complete Work, in Nine Vols.
8vo. cloth, 7*l.* 4*s.* Only a few
copies remain on hand.

CAMPBELL.--THOUGHTS
on REVELATION, with SPE-
CIAL REFERENCE to the
PRESENT TIME. By JOHN
M'LEOD CAMPBELL. Crown
8vo. 5*s.*

CAMPBELL. — THE NA-
TURE of the ATONEMENT
and its RELATION to REMIS-
SION of SINS and ETERNAL
LIFE. By JOHN M'LEOD
CAMPBELL. 8vo. 10*s.* 6*d.*

CATHERINES, The TWO ;
or, Which is the Heroine ? A
Novel. 2 vols. crown 8vo. 21*s.*

CHALLIS. — CREATION
in PLAN and in PROGRESS :
Being an Essay on the First
Chapter of Genesis. By the Rev.
JAMES CHALLIS, M.A. F.R.S.
F.R.A.S. Crown 8vo. 3*s.* 6*d.*

CHATTERTON. — LEO-
NORE: a Tale, and other Poems.
By GEORGIANA LADY
CHATTERTON. Fcap. 8vo.
cloth, 7*s.* 6*d.*

CHEYNE.—AN ELEMEN-
TARY TREATISE on the
PLANETARY THEORY. With
a Collection of Problems. By C.
H. H. CHEYNE, B.A. Crown
8vo. 6*s.* 6*d.*

CHILDE.--The SINGULAR
PROPERTIES of the ELLIP-
SOID and ASSOCIATED SUR-
FACES of the Nth DEGREE.
By the Rev. G. F. CHILDE,
M.A. 8vo. 10*s.* 6*d.*

CHRETIEN.—THE LET-
TER AND THE SPIRIT. Six
Sermons on the Inspiration of
Holy Scripture. By CHARLES
P. CHRÉTIEN. Crown 8vo. 5*s.*

CHRISTIE. — NOTES ON
BRAZILIAN QUESTIONS.
By W. D. CHRISTIE. Crown
8vo. cloth, 6*s.* 6*d.*

CICERO.—THE SECOND
PHILIPPIC ORATION. With
an Introduction and Notes, translated from Karl Halm. Edited
with corrections and additions.
By JOHN E. B. MAYOR, M.A.
Fcap. 8vo. 5*s.*

CLARA VAUGHAN. — A
Novel. 3 vols. crown 8vo. 31*s.* 6*d.*

CLARK.—FOUR SER-
MONS PREACHED IN THE
CHAPEL OF TRINITY COL-
LEGE, CAMBRIDGE. By W.
G. CLARK, M.A. Fcap. 8vo.
2*s.* 6*d.*

CLAY.—THE PRISON
CHAPLAIN. A Memoir of the
Rev. JOHN CLAY, B.D. late
Chaplain of the Preston Gaol.
With Selections from his Reports
and Correspondence, and a Sketch
of Prison-Discipline in England.
By his son, the Rev. W. L. CLAY,
M.A. 8vo. 15*s.*

CLAY.—THE POWER OF
THE KEYS. Sermons preached
in Coventry. By the Rev. W. L.
CLAY, M.A. Fcap. 8vo. 3*s.* 6*d.*

CLERGYMAN'S SELF-
EXAMINATION concerning the
APOSTLES' CREED. Extra
fcap. 8vo. 1*s.* 6*d.*

CLOUGH.—The POEMS of ARTHUR HUGH CLOUGH, sometime Fellow of Oriel College, Oxford. With a Memoir by F. T. PALGRAVE. *Second Edition.* Fcap. 8vo. 6s.

COLENSO.—WORKS by the Right Rev. J. W. COLENSO, D.D. Bishop of Natal:—

THE COLONY OF NATAL. A Journal of Visitation. With a Map and Illustrations. Fcap. 8vo. 5s.

VILLAGE SERMONS. *Second Edition.* Fcap. 8vo. 2s. 6d.

FOUR SERMONS on ORDINATION, and on MISSIONS. 18mo. 1s.

COMPANION TO THE HOLY COMMUNION, containing the Service, and Select Readings from the writings of Mr. MAURICE. *Fine Edition,* morocco, antique style, 6s. or in cloth, 2s. 6d. *Common Paper,* 1s.

ST. PAUL'S EPISTLE TO THE ROMANS. Newly Translated and Explained, from a Missionary point of View. Crown 8vo. 7s. 6d.

LETTER TO HIS GRACE THE ARCHBISHOP OF CANTERBURY, upon the Question of Polygamy, as found already existing in Converts from Heathenism. Second Edition. Crown 8vo. 1s. 6d.

COOKERY FOR ENGLISH HOUSEHOLDS. By a FRENCH LADY. Extra fcap. 8vo. 5s.

COOPER.—ATHENAE CANTABRIGIENSES. By CHARLES HENRY COOPER, F.S.A. and THOMPSON COOPER, F.S.A. Vol. I. 8vo. 1500—85, 18s. Vol. II. 1586—1609, 18s.

COTTON.—SERMONS and ADDRESSES delivered in Marlborough College during Six Years, by GEORGE EDWARD LYNCH COTTON, D.D. Lord Bishop of Calcutta. Crown 8vo. 10s. 6d.

COTTON.—A CHARGE to the CLERGY of the DIOCESE and PROVINCE of CALCUTTA at the Second Diocesan and First Metropolitan Visitation. By GEORGE EDWARD LYNCH COTTON, D.D. 8vo. 3s. 6d.

COTTON.—SERMONS: chiefly connected with Public Events of 1854. Fcap. 8vo. 3s.

COTTON.—EXPOSITORY SERMONS on the EPISTLES for the Sundays of the Christian Year. By GEORGE EDWARD LYNCH COTTON, D.D. Two Vols. crown 8vo. 15s.

CRAIK.—MY FIRST JOURNAL. A book for the Young. By GEORGIANA M. CRAIK, Author of "Riverston," "Lost and Won," &c. Royal 16mo. cloth, gilt leaves, 3s. 6d.

CROCKER.—A NEW PROPOSAL for a GEOGRAPHICAL SYSTEM of MEASURES and WEIGHTS conveniently Introducible, generally by retaining familiar notions by familiar names. To which are added remarks on systems of Coinage. By JAMES CROCKER, M.A. 8vo. 8s. 6d.

CROSSE.—AN ANALYSIS OF PALEY'S EVIDENCES. By C. H. CROSSE, M.A. 24mo. 2s. 6d.

DANTE. — DANTE'S COMEDY, *The Hell.* Translated by W. M. ROSETTI. Fcap. 8vo. cloth, 5s.

DAVIES.—ST. PAUL AND MODERN THOUGHT: Remarks on some of the Views advanced in Professor Jowett's Commentary on St. Paul. By Rev. J. LL. DAVIES, M.A. 8vo. 2s. 6d.

DAVIES.—SERMONS ON THE MANIFESTATION OF THE SON OF GOD. With a Preface addressed to Laymen on the present position of the Clergy of the Church of England; and an Appendix on the Testimony of Scripture and the Church as to the possibility of Pardon in the Future State. By the Rev. J. LL. DAVIES, M.A. Fcap. 8vo. 6s. 6d.

DAVIES.—THE WORK OF CHRIST; OR THE WORLD RECONCILED TO GOD. With a Preface on the Atonement Controversy. By the Rev. J. LL. DAVIES, M.A. Fcap. 8vo. 6s.

DAVIES.—BAPTISM, CONFIRMATION, AND THE LORD'S SUPPER, as interpreted by their outward signs. Three Expository Addresses for Parochial Use. By the Rev. J. LL. DAVIES, M.A. Limp cloth, 1s. 6d.

DAYS OF OLD : STORIES FROM OLD ENGLISH HISTORY. By the Author of "Ruth and her Friends." *New Edition.* 18mo. cloth, gilt leaves, 3s. 6d.

DEMOSTHENES DE CORONA. The Greek Text with English Notes. By B. DRAKE, M.A. *Second Edition,* to which is prefixed AESCHINES AGAINST CTESIPHON, with English Notes. Fcap. 8vo. 5s.

DE TEISSIER.—VILLAGE SERMONS, by G. F. DE TEISSIER, B.D. Crown 8vo. 9s.

SECOND SERIES. Crown 8vo. cloth. 8s. 6d.

DE VERE.—THE INFANT BRIDAL, AND OTHER POEMS. By AUBREY DE VERE. Fcap. 8vo. 7s. 6d.

DICEY. — SIX MONTHS IN THE FEDERAL STATES. By EDWARD DICEY. 2 Vols. crown 8vo. 12s.

DICEY.—ROME IN 1860. By EDWARD DICEY. Crown 8vo. 6s. 6d.

DONALDSON.—A CRITICAL HISTORY OF CHRISTIAN LITERATURE AND DOCTRINE, from the Death of the Apostles to the Nicene Council. By JAMES DONALDSON, M.A. Vol. I.—THE APOSTOLIC FATHERS. 8vo. cloth. 10s. 6d.

Vols. II. and III. in the Press.

DREW. — A GEOMETRICAL TREATISE ON CONIC SECTIONS. By W. H. DREW, M.A. *Third Edition.* Crown 8vo. 4s. 6d.

DREW.—SOLUTIONS TO PROBLEMS CONTAINED IN MR. DREW'S TREATISE ON CONIC SECTIONS. Crown 8vo. 4s. 6d.

EARLY EGYPTIAN HIS-TORY FOR THE YOUNG. With Descriptions of the Tombs and Monuments. *New Edition*, with Frontispiece. Fcap. 8vo. 5s.

ENGLISH IDYLLS. By JANE ELLICE. Fcap. 8vo. cloth. 6s.

FAWCETT.—MANUAL of POLITICAL ECONOMY. By HENRY FAWCETT, M.A. *Second Edition.* Crown 8vo. 12s.

FERRERS.—A TREATISE ON TRILINEAR CO-ORDI-NATES, the Method of Reci-procal Polars, and the Theory of Projections. By the Rev. N. M. FERRERS, M.A. Crown 8vo. 6s. 6d.

FISHER. — CONSIDERA-TIONS ON THE ORIGIN OF THE AMERICAN WAR. By HERBERT FISHER. Fcp. 8vo. 2s. 6d.

FLETCHER. — THOUGHTS FROM A GIRL'S LIFE. By LUCY FLETCHER. Fcap. 8vo. 4s. 6d.

FORBES.—LIFE OF EDWARD FORBES, F.R.S. By GEORGE WILSON, M.D. F.R.S.E. and ARCHIBALD GEIKIE, F.G.S. 8vo. with Por-trait, 14s.

FORSHALL.—THE FIRST TWELVE CHAPTERS OF THE GOSPEL ACCORDING TO ST. MATTHEW, in the Received Greek Text, with various Readings, and Notes Critical and Expository. By the late Rev. JOSIAH FORSHALL, M.A. F.R.S. 10s. 6d.

FREEMAN.—HISTORY of FEDERAL GOVERNMENT, from the Foundation of the Achaian League to the Disruption of the United States. By EDWARD A. FREEMAN, M.A. Vol. I. General Introduction. — History of the Greek Federations. 8vo. 21s.

FROST.—THE FIRST THREE SECTIONS of NEW-TON'S PRINCIPIA. With Notes and Problems in illustra-tion of the subject. By PER-CIVAL FROST, M.A. *Second Edition.* 8vo. 10s. 6d.

FROST AND WOLSTEN-HOLME.—A TREATISE ON SOLID GEOMETRY. By the Rev. PERCIVAL FROST, M.A. and the Rev. J. WOLSTEN-HOLME, M.A. 8vo. 18s.

FURNIVALL.--LE MORTE ARTHUR. Edited from the Har-leian M.S. 2252, in the British Museum. By F. J. FURNI-VALL, M.A. With Essay by the late HERBERT COLE-RIDGE. Fcap. 8vo. cloth, 7s. 6d.

GALTON.—METEORO-GRAPHICA, or Methods of Mapping the Weather. Illustrated by upwards of 600 Printed Litho-graphed Diagrams. By FRAN-CIS GALTON, F.R.S. 4to. 9s.

GARIBALDI at CAPRERA. By COLONEL VECCHJ. With Preface by Mrs. GASKILL. Fcap. 8vo. 1s. 6d.

GEIKIE.—STORY OF A BOULDER; or, Gleanings by a Field Geologist. By ARCHIBALD GEIKIE. Illustrated with Woodcuts. Crown 8vo. 5s.

GEIKIE'S SCENERY OF SCOTLAND, with Illustrations and a new Geological Map. Cr. 8vo. cloth, 10s. 6d.

GIFFORD.—THE GLORY OF GOD IN MAN. By E. H. GIFFORD, D.D. Fcap. 8vo. cloth. 3s. 6d.

GOLDEN TREASURY SERIES. Uniformly printed in 18mo. with Vignette Titles by J. NOEL PATON, T. WOOLNER, W. HOLMAN HUNT, J. E. MILLAIS, &c. Bound in extra cloth, 4s. 6d.; morocco plain, 7s. 6d.; morocco extra, 10s. 6d. each Volume.

THE GOLDEN TREASURY OF THE BEST SONGS AND LYRICAL POEMS IN THE ENGLISH LANGUAGE. Selected and arranged, with Notes, by FRANCIS TURNER PALGRAVE.

THE CHILDREN'S GARLAND FROM THE BEST POETS. Selected and arranged by COVENTRY PATMORE.

THE BOOK OF PRAISE. From the best English Hymn Writers. Selected and arranged by ROUNDELL PALMER. A New and Enlarged Edition.

THE FAIRY BOOK : The Best Popular Fairy Stories. Selected and Rendered Anew by the Author of " John Halifax."

THE BALLAD BOOK. A Selection of the Choicest British Ballads. Edited by WILLIAM ALLINGHAM.

THE JEST BOOK. The Choicest Anecdotes and Sayings. Selected and arranged by MARK LEMON.

BACON'S ESSAYS AND COLOURS OF GOOD AND EVIL. With Notes and Glossarial Index, by W. ALDIS WRIGHT, M.A. Large paper copies, crown 8vo. 7s. 6d.; or bound in half morocco, 10s. 6d.

The PILGRIM'S PROGRESS from this World to that which is to Come. By JOHN BUNYAN.

⁎ Large paper Copies, crown 8vo. cloth, 7s. 6d.; or bound in half morocco, 10s. 6d.

THE SUNDAY BOOK OF POETRY FOR THE YOUNG. Selected and arranged by C. F. ALEXANDER.

A BOOK OF GOLDEN DEEDS OF ALL TIMES AND ALL COUNTRIES. Gathered and Narrated anew by the Author of " The Heir of Redclyffe."

THE POETICAL WORKS OF ROBERT BURNS. Edited, with Biographical Memoir, by ALEXANDER SMITH. 2 vols.

GORDON. — LETTERS from EGYPT, 1863—5. By LADY DUFF GORDON. Cr. 8vo. cloth, 8s. 6d.

GORST.—THE MAORI KING; or, the Story of our Quarrel with the Natives of New Zealand. By J. E. GORST, M.A. With a Portrait of William Thompson, and a Map of the Seat of War. Crown 8vo. 10s. 6d.

GROVES.—A COMMEN-
TARY ON THE BOOK OF
GENESIS. For the Use of Stu-
dents and Readers of the English
Version of the Bible. By the
Rev. H. C. GROVES, M.A.
Crown 8vo. 9s.

GUIDE TO THE UNPRO-
TECTED in Every Day Mat-
ters relating to Property and
Income. By a BANKER'S
DAUGHTER. *Second Edition.*
Extra fcap. 8vo. 3s. 6d.

HAMERTON.—A PAINT-
ER'S CAMP IN THE HIGH-
LANDS; and Thoughts about
Art. By P. G. HAMERTON.
2 vols. crown 8vo. 21s.

HAMILTON. — THE RE-
SOURCES OF A NATION.
A Series of Essays. By ROW-
LAND HAMILTON. 8vo.
10s. 6d.

HAMILTON.—On TRUTH
and ERROR: Thoughts on the
Principles of Truth, and the
Causes and Effects of Error. By
JOHN HAMILTON. Crown
8vo. 5s.

HARDWICK.—CHRIST
AND OTHER MASTERS. A
Historical Inquiry into some of
the Chief Parallelisms and Con-
trasts between Christianity and the
Religious Systems of the Ancient
World. By the Ven. ARCH-
DEACON HARDWICK. *New
Edition,* revised, and a Prefato
Memoir by the Rev. FRANCIS
PROCTER. Two vols. crown
8vo. 15s.

HARDWICK. — A HIS-
TORY OF THE CHRISTIAN
CHURCH, during the Middle
Ages and the Reformation. (A.D.
590—1600.) By ARCHDEACON
HARDWICK. Two vols. crown
8vo. 21s.
   Vol. I. *Second Edition.* Edited
by FRANCIS PROCTER, M.A.
History from Gregory the Great to
the Excommunication of Luther.
With Maps.
   Vol. II. History of the Refor-
mation of the Church.
   Each volume may be had sepa-
rately. Price 10s. 6d.

HARDWICK. — TWENTY
SERMONS FOR TOWN CON-
GREGATIONS. Crown 8vo.
6s. 6d.

HARE.—WORKS BY
JULIUS CHARLES HARE,
M.A. Sometime Archdeacon of
Lewes, and Chaplain in Ordi-
nary to the Queen.

CHARGES DELIVERED
during the Years 1840 to 1854.
With Notes on the Principal
Events affecting the Church
during that period. With an
Introduction, explanatory of his
position in the Church with reference to the parties which divide
it. 3 vols. 8vo. 1l. 11s. 6d.

MISCELLANEOUS PAM-
PHLETS on some of the Leading
Questions agitated in the Church
during the Years 1845—51. 8vo.
12s.

THE VICTORY OF FAITH.
New Edition, in the press, with
Life by Plumptre.

THE MISSION OF THE COM-
FORTER. *Third Edition.* With
Notes, 12s.

VINDICATION OF LUTHER. *Second Edition.* 8vo. 7*s.*

PARISH SERMONS. Second Series. 8vo. cloth, 12*s.*

SERMONS PREACHED ON PARTICULAR OCCASIONS. 8vo. cloth, 12*s.*

PORTIONS OF THE PSALMS IN ENGLISH VERSE. Selected for Public Worship. 18mo. cloth, 2*s.* 6*d.*

** The two following Books are included in the Three Volumes of Charges, but may be had separately.

THE CONTEST WITH ROME. *Second Edition.* 8vo. cl. 10*s.* 6*d.*

CHARGES DELIVERED in the Years 1843, 1845, 1846. With an Introduction. 6*s.* 6*d.*

HEARN. — PLUTOLOGY; or, the Theory of the Efforts to Satisfy Human Wants. By W. E. HEARN, LL.D. 8vo. 14*s.*

HEBERT. — CLERICAL SUBSCRIPTION, an Inquiry into the Real Position of the Church and the Clergy in reference to — I. The Articles; II. The Liturgy; III. The Canons and Statutes. By the Rev. CHARLES HEBERT, M.A. F.R.S.L. Cr. 8vo. 7*s.* 6*d.*

HEMMING. — AN ELEMENTARY TREATISE ON THE DIFFERENTIAL AND INTEGRAL CALCULUS. By G. W. HEMMING, M.A. *Second Edition.* 8vo. 9*s.*

HERVEY. — THE GENEALOGIES OF OUR LORD AND SAVIOUR JESUS CHRIST, as contained in the Gospels of St. Matthew and St. Luke, reconciled with each other, and shown to be in harmony with the true Chronology of the Times. By Lord ARTHUR HERVEY, M.A. 8vo. 10*s.* 6*d.*

HERVEY. — THE AARBERGS. By ROSAMOND HERVEY. 2 vols. crown 8vo. cloth, 21*s.*

HISTORICUS. — LETTERS ON SOME QUESTIONS OF INTERNATIONAL LAW. Reprinted from the *Times*, with considerable Additions. 8vo. 7*s.* 6*d.* Also, ADDITIONAL LETTERS. 8vo. 2*s.* 6*d.*

HODGSON. — MYTHOLOGY FOR LATIN VERSIFICATION: a Brief Sketch of the Fables of the Ancients, prepared to be rendered into Latin Verse for Schools. By F. HODGSON, B.D. late Provost of Eton. New Edition, revised by F. C. HODGSON, M.A. 18mo. 3*s.*

HORNER. — The TUSCAN POET GIUSEPPE GIUSTI AND HIS TIMES. By SUSAN HORNER. Crown 8vo. 7*s.* 6*d.*

HOWARD. — THE PENTATEUCH; or, the Five Books of Moses. Translated into English from the Version of the LXX. With Notes on its Omissions and Insertions, and also on the Passages in which it differs from the Authorized Version. By the Hon. HENRY HOWARD, D.D. Crown 8vo. GENESIS, 1 vol. 8*s.* 6*d.*; EXODUS AND LEVITICUS, 1 vol. 10*s.* 6*d.*; NUMBERS AND DEUTERONOMY, 1 vol. 10*s.* 6*d.*

HUMPHRY.—THE HUMAN SKELETON (including the JOINTS). By GEORGE MURRAY HUMPHRY, M.D. F.R.S. With Two Hundred and Sixty Illustrations drawn from Nature. Medium 8vo. 1*l*. 8*s.*

HUMPHRY.—THE HUMAN HAND AND THE HUMAN FOOT. With Numerous Illustrations. Fcp. 8vo. 4*s.* 6*d.*

HYDE.—HOW TO WIN OUR WORKERS. An Account of the Leeds Sewing School. By Mrs. HYDE. Fcap. 8vo. 1*s.* 6*d.*

HYMNI ECCLESIÆ.— Fcap. 8vo. cloth, 7*s.* 6*d.*

JAMESON.—LIFE'S WORK, IN PREPARATION AND IN RETROSPECT. Sermons Preached before the University of Cambridge. By the Rev. F. J. JAMESON, M.A. Fcap. 8vo. 1*s.* 6*d.*

JAMESON.—BROTHERLY COUNSELS TO STUDENTS. Sermons preached in the Chapel of St. Catharine's College, Cambridge. By F. J. JAMESON, M.A. Fcap. 8vo. 1*s.* 6*d.*

JANET'S HOME.—A Novel. *New Edition.* Crown 8vo. 6*s.*

JEVONS.—THE COAL QUESTION. ByW.STANLEY JEVONS, M.A. Fellow of University College, London. 8vo. 10*s.* 6*d.*

JONES.—THE CHURCH of ENGLAND and COMMON SENSE. By HARRY JONES, M.A. Fcap. 8vo. cloth, 3*s.* 6*d.*

JUVENAL.—JUVENAL, for Schools. With English Notes. By J. E. B. MAYOR, M.A. *New and Cheaper Edition.* Crown 8vo. *Reprinting.*

KEARY'S THE LITTLE WANDERLING, and other Fairy Tales. 18mo cloth, 3*s.* 6*d.*

KINGSLEY.—WORKS BY THE REV. CHARLES KINGSLEY, M.A. Rector of Eversley, and Professor of Modern History in the University of Cambridge :—

THE ROMAN and the TEUTON. A Series of Lectures delivered before the University of Cambridge. 8vo. 12*s.*

TWO YEARS AGO. *Third Edition.* Crown 8vo. 6*s.*

"WESTWARD HO!" *Fourth Edition.* Crown 8vo. 6*s.*

ALTON LOCKE. *New Edition.* with a New Preface. Crown 8vo. 4*s.* 6*d.*

HYPATIA; *Fourth Edition.* Crn. 8vo. 6*s.*

YEAST. *Fourth Edition.* Fcap. 8vo. 5*s.*

MISCELLANIES. *Second Edition.* 2 vols. crown 8vo. 12*s.*

THE SAINT'S TRAGEDY. *Third Edition.* Fcap. 8vo. 5*s.*

ANDROMEDA, and other Poems. *Third Edition.* Fcap. 8vo. 5*s.*

THE WATER BABIES, a Fairy Tale for a Land Baby. With Two Illustrations by J. NOEL PATON, R.S.A. *New Edition.* Crown 8vo. 6*s.*

GLAUCUS: or, the Wonders of the Shore. *New and Illustrated Edition*, containing beautifully Coloured Illustrations. 5s.

THE HEROES; or, Greek Fairy Tales for my Children. With Eight Illustrations. *New Edition.* 18mo. 3s. 6d.

VILLAGE SERMONS. *Sixth Edition.* Fcap. 8vo. 2s. 6d.

THE GOSPEL OF THE PENTATEUCH. *Second Edition.* Fcap. 8vo. 4s. 6d.

GOOD NEWS OF GOD. *Third Edition.* Fcap. 8vo. 6s.

SERMONS FOR THE TIMES. *Third Edition.* Fcap. 8vo. 3s. 6d.

TOWN AND COUNTRY SERMONS. Fcap. 8vo. 6s.

SERMONS ON NATIONAL SUBJECTS. First Series. *Second Edition.* Fcap. 8vo. 5s.

SERMONS ON NATIONAL SUBJECTS. Second Series. *Second Edition.* Fcap. 8vo. 5s.

ALEXANDRIA AND HER SCHOOLS. With a Preface. Crown 8vo. 5s.

THE LIMITS OF EXACT SCIENCE AS APPLIED TO HISTORY. An Inaugural Lecture delivered before the University of Cambridge. Crown 8vo. 2s.

PHAETHON; or Loose Thoughts for Loose Thinkers. *Third Edition.* Crown 8vo. 2s.

DAVID.—Four Sermons—David's Weakness—David's Strength—David's Anger—David's Deserts. Fcap. 8vo. cloth, 2s. 6d.

KINGSLEY. — AUSTIN ELLIOT. By HENRY KINGSLEY, Author of "Ravenshoe," &c. *Third Edition.* 2 vols. crown 8vo. 21s.

KINGSLEY. — THE RECOLLECTIONS OF GEOFREY HAMLYN. By HENRY KINGSLEY. *Second Edition.* Crown 8vo. 6s.

KINGSLEY.—THE HILLYARS AND THE BURTONS: a Story of Two Families. By HENRY KINGSLEY. 3 vols. crown 8vo. cloth, 1l. 11s. 6d.

KINGSLEY.—RAVENSHOE. By HENRY KINGSLEY. *New Edition.* Crown 8vo. 6s.

KINGTON.—HISTORY of FREDERICK the SECOND, Emperor of the Romans. By T. L. KINGTON, M.A. 2 vols. demy 8vo. 32s.

KIRCHHOFF. — RESEARCHES on the SOLAR SPECTRUM and the SPECTRA of the CHEMICAL ELEMENTS. By G. KIRCHHOFF, of Heidelberg. Translated by HENRY E. ROSCOE, B.A. 4to. 5s. Also the Second Part. 4to. 5s. with 2 Plates.

LANCASTER —ECLOGUES AND MONO-DRAMAS; or, a Collection of Verses. By WILLIAM LANCASTER. Extra fcap. 8vo. 4s. 6d.

LANCASTER. — PRÆTERITA: Poems. By WILLIAM LANCASTER. Extra fcap. 8vo. 4s. 6d.

LATHAM. — THE CON-
STRUCTION of WROUGHT-
IRON BRIDGES, embracing the
Practical Application of the Prin-
ciples of Mechanics to Wrought-
Iron Girder Work. By J. H.
LATHAM, Esq. Civil Engineer.
8vo. With numerous detail Plates.
Second Edition. [*Preparing.*

LECTURES TO LADIES
ON PRACTICAL SUBJECTS.
Third Edition, revised. Crown
8vo. 7s. 6d.

LEMON. — LEGENDS OF
NUMBER NIP. By MARK
LEMON. With Six Illustra-
tions by CHARLES KEENE. Extra
fcap. 5s.

LESLEY'S GUARDIANS:
A Novel. By CECIL HOME.
3 vols. crown 8vo. 31s. 6d.

LIGHTFOOT. — ST.
PAUL'S EPISTLE TO THE
GALATIANS. A Revised Text,
with Notes and Dissertations.
By J. D. LIGHTFOOT, D.D.
8vo. cloth, 10s. 6d.

LOWELL. — FIRESIDE
TRAVELS. By JAMES RUS-
SELL LOWELL, Author of
"The Biglow Papers." Fcap.
8vo. 4s. 6d.

LUDLOW and HUGHES.—
A SKETCH of the HISTORY
of the UNITED STATES from
Independence to Secession. By
J. M. LUDLOW, Author of
"British India, its Races and its
History," "The Policy of the
Crown towards India," &c.
   To which is added, THE
STRUGGLE FOR KANSAS.
By THOMAS HUGHES, Author
of "Tom Brown's School Days,"
"Tom Brown at Oxford," &c.
Crown 8vo. 8s. 6d.

LUDLOW. — BRITISH
INDIA; its Races, and its History, down to 1857. By JOHN
MALCOLM LUDLOW, Bar-
rister-at-Law. 2 vols. 9s.

LUSHINGTON. — THE
ITALIAN WAR 1848-9, and
the Last Italian Poet. By the
late HENRY LUSHINGTON.
With a Biographical Preface by
G. S. VENABLES. Crown 8vo.
6s. 6d.

LYTTELTON. — THE
COMUS OF MILTON rendered
into Greek Verse. By LORD
LYTTELTON. Royal fcap. 8vo.
5s.

MACKENZIE. — THE
CHRISTIAN CLERGY of the
FIRST TEN CENTURIES,
and their Influence on European
Civilization. By HENRY MAC-
KENZIE, B.A. Scholar of Trinity
College, Cambridge. Crown 8vo.
6s. 6d.

MACLAREN. — SERMONS
PREACHED AT MANCHES-
TER. By ALEXANDER MAC-
LAREN. *Second Edition.* Fcp.
8vo. 4s. 6d.

MACLEAR. — A HISTORY
OF CHRISTIAN MISSIONS
DURING THE MIDDLE
AGES. By G. F. MACLEAR,
M.A. Crown 8vo. 10s 6d.

MACLEAR. — THE WIT-
NESS OF THE EUCHARIST;
or, The Institution and Early
Celebration of the Lord's Supper,
considered as an Evidence of the
Historical Truth of the Gospel
Narrative and of the Atonement.
Crown 8vo. 4s. 6d.

MACLEAR. — A CLASS-DOOK OF OLD TESTAMENT HISTORY. By the Rev. G. F. MACLEAR, M.A. With Four Maps. 18mo. cloth, 4s. 6d.

MACLEAR. — A CLASS-BOOK OF NEW TESTAMENT HISTORY, including the connexion of the Old and New Testament.

[*In the press.*

MACMILLAN. — FOOT-NOTES FROM THE PAGE OF NATURE. By the Rev. HUGH MACMILLAN, F.R.S.E. With numerous Illustrations. Fcap. 8vo. 5s.

MACMILLAN'S MAGAZINE. Published Monthly, price One Shilling. Volumes I.--XI. are now ready, 7s. 6d. each.

McCOSH.—The METHOD of the DIVINE GOVERNMENT, Physical and Moral. By JAMES McCOSH, LL.D. *Eighth Edition.* 8vo. 10s. 6d.

McCOSH.—THE SUPERNATURAL IN RELATION TO THE NATURAL. By JAMES McCOSH, LL.D. Crown 8vo. 7s. 6d.

McCOSH. — THE INTUITIONS OF THE MIND. By JAMES McCOSH, LL.D. *A New Edition.* 8vo. cloth, 10s. 6d.

McCOY.—CONTRIBUTIONS TO BRITISH PALÆONTOLOGY; or, First Descriptions of several hundred Fossil Radiata, Articulata, Mollusca, and Pisces, from the Tertiary, Cretaceous, Oolitic, and Palæozoic Strata of Great Britain. With numerous Woodcuts. By FRED. McCOY, F.G.S. Professor of Natural History in the University of Melbourne. 8vo. 9s.

MANSFIELD. — PARAGUAY, BRAZIL, AND THE PLATE. With a Map, and numerous Woodcuts. By CHARLES MANSFIELD, M.A. With a Sketch of his Life. By the Rev. CHARLES KINGSLEY. Crown 8vo. 12s. 6d.

MARRIED BENEATH HIM. By the Author of "Lost Sir Massingberd." 3 vols. crown 8vo. cloth, 1l. 11s. 6d.

MARRINER. — SERMONS PREACHED at LYME REGIS. By E. T. MARRINER, Curate. Fcap. 8vo. 4s. 6d.

MARSTON.—A LADY IN HER OWN RIGHT. By WESTLAND MARSTON. Crown 8vo. 6s.

MARTIN.—THE STATESMAN'S YEAR BOOK for 1865. A Statistical, Genealogical, and Historical Account of the Civilized World for the Year 1865. By FREDERICK MARTIN. Cr. 8vo. 10s. 6d.

MARTIN. — STORIES OF BANKS AND BANKERS. By FREDERICK MARTIN. Fcp. 8vo. cloth, 3s. 6d.

MARTIN.—THE LIFE OF JOHN CLARE. By FREDERICK MARTIN. Crown 8vo. cloth, 7s. 6d.

MASSON.—ESSAYS, BIOGRAPHICAL and CRITICAL; chiefly on the English Poets. By DAVID MASSON, M.A. 8vo. 12s. 6d.

MASSON.—BRITISH NOVELISTS AND THEIR STYLES; being a Critical Sketch of the History of British Prose Fiction. By DAVID MASSON, M.A. Crown 8vo. 7s. 6d.

MASSON.—LIFE of JOHN MILTON, narrated in Connexion with the Political, Ecclesiastical, and Literary History of his Time. Vol. I. with Portraits. 18s.

MASSON.—RECENT BRITISH PHILOSOPHY. A Review, with Criticisms. By DAVID MASSON. Crown 8vo. cloth, 7s. 6d.

MAURICE.—WORKS BY THE REV. FREDERICK DENISON MAURICE, M.A.

THE CLAIMS OF THE BIBLE AND OF SCIENCE; a Correspondence on some questions respecting the Pentateuch. Crown 8vo. 4s. 6d.

DIALOGUES on FAMILY WORSHIP. Crown 8vo. 6s.

EXPOSITORY DISCOURSES on the Holy Scriptures :—
THE PATRIARCHS and LAWGIVERS of the OLD TESTAMENT. *Second Edition.* Crown 8vo. 6s.
This volume contains Discourses on the Pentateuch, Joshua, Judges, and the beginning of the First Book of Samuel.

THE PROPHETS and KINGS of the OLD TESTAMENT. *Second Edition.* Crown 8vo. 10s. 6d.
This volume contains Discourses on Samuel I. and II., Kings I. and II. Amos, Joel, Hosea, Isaiah, Micah, Nahum, Habakkuk, Jeremiah, and Ezekiel.

THE GOSPEL OF THE KINGDOM OF GOD. A Series of Lectures on the Gospel of St. Luke. Crown 8vo. 9s.

THE GOSPEL OF ST. JOHN ; a Series of Discourses. *Second Edition.* Crown 8vo. 10s. 6d.

THE EPISTLES OF ST. JOHN ; a Series of Lectures on Christian Ethics. Crown 8vo. 7s. 6d.

EXPOSITORY SERMONS ON THE PRAYER-BOOK :—
THE ORDINARY SERVICES. *Second Edition.* Fcap. 8vo. 5s. 6d.
THE CHURCH A FAMILY. Twelve Sermons on the Occasional Services. Fcap. 8vo. 4s. 6d.

LECTURES ON THE APOCALYPSE, or, Book of the Revelation of St. John the Divine. Crown 8vo. 10s. 6d.

WHAT IS REVELATION ? A Series of Sermons on the Epiphany, to which are added Letters to a Theological Student on the Bampton Lectures of Mr. MANSEL. Crown 8vo. 10s. 6d.

SEQUEL TO THE INQUIRY, "WHAT IS REVELATION?" Letters in Reply to Mr. Mansel's Examination of "Strictures on the Bampton Lectures." Crown 8vo. 6s.

LECTURES ON ECCLESIASTICAL HISTORY. 8vo. 10s. 6d.

THEOLOGICAL ESSAYS. *Second Edition.* Crown 8vo. 10s. 6d.

THE DOCTRINE OF SACRIFICE DEDUCED FROM THE SCRIPTURES. Cr. 8vo. 7s. 6d.

THE RELIGIONS OF THE WORLD, and their Relations to Christianity. *Fourth Edition.* Fcap. 8vo. 5s.

ON THE LORD'S PRAYER. *Fourth Edition.* Fcap. 8vo. 2s. 6d.

ON THE SABBATH DAY; the Character of the Warrior; and on the Interpretation of History. Fcap. 8vo. 2s. 6d.

LEARNING AND WORKING. —Six Lectures on the Foundation of Colleges for Working Men. Crown 8vo. 5s.

THE INDIAN CRISIS. Five Sermons. Crown 8vo. 2s. 6d.

LAW'S REMARKS ON THE FABLE OF THE BEES. With an Introduction by F. D. MAURICE, M.A. Fcap. 8vo. 4s. 6d.

MAYOR.—AUTOBIOGRAPHY OF MATTHEW ROBINSON. By JOHN E. B. MAYOR, M.A. Fcp. 8vo. 5s. 6d.

MAYOR. — EARLY STATUTES of ST. JOHN'S COLLEGE, CAMBRIDGE. With Notes. Royal 8vo. 18s.

MELIBŒUS IN LONDON. By JAMES PAYN, M.A. Fcap. 8vo. 2s. 6d.

MERIVALE. — SALLUST FOR SCHOOLS. By C. MERIVALE, B.D. *Second Edition.* Fcap. 8vo. 4s. 6d.

⁎ The Jugurtha and the Catalina may be had separately, price 2s. 6d. each.

MERIVALE.—KEATS' HYPERION Rendered into Latin Verse. By C. MERIVALE, B.D. *Second Edition.* Royal fcap. 8vo. 3s. 6d.

MOOR COTTAGE.—A Tale of Home Life. By the Author of " Little Estella." Crown 8vo. 6s.

MOORHOUSE. — SOME MODERN DIFFICULTIES respecting the FACTS of NATURE and REVELATION. By JAMES MOORHOUSE, M.A. Fcap. 8vo. 2s. 6d.

MORGAN. — A COLLECTION OF MATHEMATICAL PROBLEMS and EXAMPLES. By H. A. MORGAN, M.A. Crown 8vo. 6s. 6d.

MORSE.—WORKING FOR GOD, and other Practical Sermons. By FRANCIS MORSE, M.A. *Second Edition.* Fcap. 8vo. 5s.

MORTLOCK. — CHRISTIANITY AGREEABLE TO REASON. By the Rev. EDMUND MORTLOCK, B.D. *Second Edition.* Fcap. 8vo. 3s. 6d.

NOEL.—BEHIND THE VEIL, and other Poems. By the Hon. RODEN NOEL. Fcap. 8vo. 7s.

NORTHERN CIRCUIT. Brief Notes of Travel in Sweden, Finland, and Russia. With a Frontispiece. Crown 8vo. 5s.

NORTON.—THE LADY of LA GARAYE. By the Hon. Mrs. NORTON. With Vignette and Frontispiece. *New Edition.* 4s. 6d.

O'BRIEN.—An ATTEMPT to EXPLAIN and ESTABLISH the DOCTRINE of JUSTIFICATION BY FAITH ONLY. By JAMES THOS. O'BRIEN, D.D. Bishop of Ossory. *Third Edition.* 8vo. 12s.

O'BRIEN.—CHARGE delivered at the Visitation in 1863. *Second Edition.* 8vo. 2s.

OLIPHANT.—AGNES HOPETOUN'S SCHOOLS AND HOLIDAYS. By MRS. OLIPHANT. Royal 16mo. cloth, gilt leaves. 3s. 6d.

OLIVER. — LESSONS IN ELEMENTARY BOTANY. With nearly 200 Illustrations. By DANIEL OLIVER, F.R.S. F.L.S. 18mo. 4s. 6d.

OPPEN.—FRENCH READER, for the Use of Colleges and Schools. By EDWARD A. OPPEN. Fcap. 8vo. cloth, 4s. 6d.

ORWELL.—The BISHOP'S WALK AND THE BISHOP'S TIMES. Poems on the Days of Archbishop Leighton and the Scottish Covenant. By ORWELL. Fcap. 8vo. 5s.

OUR YEAR. — A Child's Book, in Prose and Verse. By the Author of "John Halifax, Gentleman." Illustrated by CLARENCE DOVELL. Royal 16mo. cloth, 3s. 6d.

PALGRAVE.—HISTORY OF NORMANDY AND OF ENGLAND. By Sir FRANCIS PALGRAVE. Completing the History to the Death of William Rufus. Vols. I. to IV. 8vo. each 21s.

PALGRAVE.—A NARRATIVE OF A YEAR'S JOURNEY THROUGH CENTRAL AND EASTERN ARABIA, 1862–3. By WILLIAM GIFFARD PALGRAVE (late of the Eighth Regiment Bombay N.I.). 2 vols. 8vo. cloth. 28s.

PALMER.—THE BOOK of PRAISE : from the Best English Hymn Writers. Selected and arranged by ROUNDELL PALMER. With Vignette by WOOLNER. *Large Type Edition*, demy 8vo. 10s. 6d. ; morocco, 28s. *Royal Edition*, crown 8vo. 6s. ; morocco, 12s. 6d.

PARKINSON.—A TREATISE ON ELEMENTARY MECHANICS. For the Use of the Junior Classes at the University and the Higher Classes in Schools. With a Collection of Examples. By S. PARKINSON, B.D. *Third Edition*, revised. Crown 8vo. 9s. 6d.

PARKINSON.—A TREATISE ON OPTICS. By S. PARKINSON, B.D. Crown 8vo. 10s. 6d.

PATERSON. — TREATISE ON THE FISHERY LAWS of the UNITED KINGDOM, including the Laws of Angling. By JAMES PATERSON, M.A. Crown 8vo. 10s.

PATMORE.—The ANGEL IN THE HOUSE. Book I. The Betrothal.—Book II. The Espousals.—Book III. Faithful for Ever. With Tamerton Church Tower. By COVENTRY PATMORE. 2 vols. fcap. 8vo. 12s.

B

PATMORE. — THE VIC-
TORIES OF LOVE. Fcap.
8vo. 4s. 6d.

PAULI. — PICTURES OF
OLD ENGLAND. By Dr.
REINHOLD PAULI. Trans-
lated by E. C. OTTE. Crown
8vo. 8s. 6d.

PEEL.—JUDAS MACCA-
BÆUS. An Heroic Poem. By
EDMUND PEEL. Fcap. 8vo.
7s. 6d.

PHEAR.—ELEMENTARY
HYDROSTATICS. By J. B.
PHEAR, M.A. *Third Edition.*
Crown 8vo. 5s. 6d.

PHILLIMORE.–PRIVATE
LAW among the ROMANS.
From the Pandects. By JOHN
GEORGE PHILLIMORE, Q.C.
8vo. 16s.

PHILLIPS.—LIFE on the
EARTH : its Origin and Succes-
sion. By JOHN PHILLIPS,
M.A. LL.D. F.R.S. With Illustrations. Crown 8vo. 6s. 6d.

PHILOLOGY.—The JOUR-
NAL OF SACRED AND
CLASSICAL PHILOLOGY.
Four vols. 8vo. 12s. 6d. each.

PLATO.—The REPUBLIC
OF PLATO. Translated into
English, with Notes. By Two
Fellows of Trinity College, Cam-
bridge (J. Ll. Davies, M.A. and
D. J. Vaughan, M.A.). *Second
Edition.* 8vo. 10s. 6d.

PLATONIC DIALOGUES,
The. For English Readers. By
W. WHEWELL, D.D. F.R.S.
Master of Trinity College, Cambridge. Vol. I. *Second Edition,*
containing *The Socratic Dialogues,*
fcap. 8vo. 7s. 6d. Vol. II. containing *The Anti-Sophist Dialogues,* 6s. 6d. Vol. III. containing *The Republic,* fcap. 8vo.
7s. 6d.

PLEA for a NEW ENGLISH
VERSION of THE SCRIP-
TURES. By a Licentiate of the
Church of Scotland. 8vo. 6s.

POTTER.—A VOICE from
the CHURCH in AUSTRA-
LIA : Sermons preached in Melbourne. By the Rev. ROBERT
POTTER, M.A. Royal fcap.
8vo. 4s. 6d.

PRATT.—TREATISE ON
ATTRACTIONS, La Place's
FUNCTIONS, and the FIGURE
of the EARTH. By J. H.
PRATT, M.A. *Second Edition.*
Crown 8vo. 6s. 6d.

PROCTER.—A HISTORY
of the BOOK OF COMMON
PRAYER : with a Rationale of
its Offices. By FRANCIS
PROCTER, M.A. *Fifth Edi-
tion,* revised and enlarged. Cr.
8vo. 10s. 6d.

PROCTER.—An ELEMEN-
TARY HISTORY of the BOOK
of COMMON PRAYER. By
FRANCIS PROCTER, M.A.
18mo. 2s. 6d.

PROPERTY and INCOME.
—GUIDE to the UNPROTEC-
TED in Matters relating to Property and Income. *Second Edition.* Crown 8vo. 3s. 6d.

PUCKLE.—AN ELEMEN-TARY TREATISE on CONIC SECTIONS and ALGEBRAIC GEOMETRY, especially designed for the Use of Schools and Beginners. By G. HALE PUCKLE, M.A. *Second Edition.* Crown 8vo. 7s. 6d.

RAMSAY. — THE CATE-CHISER'S MANUAL; or, the Church Catechism illustrated and explained, for the Use of Clergymen, Schoolmasters, and Teachers. By ARTHUR RAMSAY, M.A. *Second Edition.* 18mo. 1s. 6d.

RAWLINSON.—ELEMEN-TARY STATICS. By G. RAWLINSON, M.A. Edited by EDWARD STURGES, M.A. Crown 8vo. 4s. 6d.

RAYS of SUNLIGHT for DARK DAYS. A Book of Selections for the Suffering. With a Preface by C. J. VAUGHAN, D.D. 18mo. *New Edition.* 3s. 6d.; morocco, old style, 9s.

ROBERTS.—DISCUS-SIONS ON THE GOSPELS. By REV. ALEXANDER RO-BERTS, D.D. *Second Edition.* revised and enlarged. 8vo. cloth, 16s.

ROBY. — AN ELEMEN-TARY LATIN GRAMMAR. By H. J. ROBY, M.A. 18mo. 2s. 6d.

ROBY.—STORY OF A HOUSEHOLD, and Other Poems. By MARY K. ROBY, Fcap. 8vo. 5s.

ROMANIS.—SERMONS PREACHED at ST. MARY'S, READING. By WILLIAM ROMANIS, M.A. *First Series.* Fcap. 8vo. 6s. Also, *Second Series.* 6s.

ROSSETTI.—GOBLIN MARKET, and other Poems. By CHRISTINA ROSSETTI. With Two Designs by D. G. ROSSETTI. *Second Edition.* Fcap. 8vo. 5s.

ROSSETTI. — THE PRINCE'S PROGRESS, and other Poems. By CHRISTINA ROSSETTI. With Two Designs by D. G. ROSSETTI. *In the press.*

ROSSETTI. — DANTE'S COMEDY: *The Hell.* Translated into Literal Blank Verse. By W. M. ROSSETTI. Fcap. 8vo. cloth. 5s.

ROUTH.—TREATISE ON DYNAMICS OF RIGID BO-DIES. With Numerous Examples. By E. J. ROUTH, M.A. Crown 8vo. 10s. 6d.

ROWSELL.—The ENGLISH UNIVERSITIES AND THE ENGLISH POOR. Sermons preached before the University of Cambridge. By T. J. ROW-SELL, M.A. Fcap. 8vo. 2s.

ROWSELL. — MAN'S LABOUR and GOD'S HAR-VEST. Sermons preached before the University of Cambridge in Lent, 1861. Fcap. 8vo. 3s.

RUFFINI. — VINCENZO; or, SUNKEN ROCKS. By JOHN RUFFINI. Three vols. crown 8vo. 31s. 6d.

RUTH and her FRIENDS. A Story for Girls. With a Frontispiece. *Fourth Edition.* Royal 16mo. 3s. 6d.

SCOURING of the WHITE HORSE; or, the Long Vacation Ramble of a London Clerk. By the Author of "Tom Brown's School Days." Illustrated by DOYLE. *Eighth Thousand.* Imp. 16mo. 8s. 6d.

SEEMANN.—VITI: an Account of a Government Mission to the Vitian or Fijian Group of Islands. By BERTHOLD SEEMANN, Ph.D. F.L.S. With Map and Illustrations. Demy 8vo. 14s.

SELWYN.—THE WORK of CHRIST in the WORLD. By G. A. SELWYN, D.D. *Third Edition.* Crown 8vo. 2s.

SHAKESPEARE.—THE WORKS OF WILLIAM SHAKESPEARE. Edited by WM. GEORGE CLARK, M.A. and W. ALDIS WRIGHT, M.A. Vols. 1 to 6, 8vo. 10s. 6d. each. To be completed in Eight Volumes.

SHAKESPEARE.—THE COMPLETE WORKS OF WILLIAM SHAKESPEARE. The *Globe Edition.* Edited by W. G. CLARK and W. A. WRIGHT. Royal Fcap. 3s. 6d.

SHAKESPEARE'S TEMPEST. With Glossarial and Explanatory Notes. By the Rev. J. M. JEPHSON. 18mo. 3s. 6d.

SHAIRP. — KILMAHOE: and other Poems. By J. CAMPBELL SHAIRP. Fcap. 8vo. 5s.

SHIRLEY.—ELIJAH; Four University Sermons. I. Samaria. II. Carmel.—III. Kishon.—IV. Horeb. By W. W. SHIRLEY, D.D. Fcap. 8vo. 2s. 6d.

SIMEON.—STRAY NOTES ON FISHING AND ON NATURAL HISTORY. By CORNWALL SIMEON. Cr. 8vo. 7s. 6d.

SIMPSON.—AN EPITOME OF THE HISTORY OF THE CHRISTIAN CHURCH. By WILLIAM SIMPSON, M.A. *Fourth Edition.* Fcp. 8vo. 3s. 6d.

SKETCHES FROM CAMBRIDGE. By A DON. Crown 8vo. cloth, 3s. 6d.

SMITH.—A LIFE DRAMA, and other Poems. By ALEXANDER SMITH. Fcap. 8vo. 2s. 6d.

SMITH. — CITY POEMS. By ALEXANDER SMITH, Fcap. 8vo. 5s.

SMITH.—EDWIN OF DEIRA. *Second Edition.* By ALEXANDER SMITH. Fcap. 8vo. 5s.

SMITH.—A LETTER TO A WHIG MEMBER of the SOUTHERN INDEPENDENCE ASSOCIATION. Ey GOLDWIN SMITH. Extra fcap. 8vo. 2s.

SMITH. — ARITHMETIC AND ALGEBRA. By BARNARD SMITH, M.A. *Ninth Edition.* Cr. 8vo. cloth, 10s. 6d.

SMITH. — ARITHMETIC for the USE of SCHOOLS. *New Edition.* Crown 8vo. 4s. 6d

SMITH.—A KEY to the ARITHMETIC for SCHOOLS. *Second Edition.* Crown 8vo. 8*s.* 6*d.*

SMITH.—EXERCISES IN ARITHMETIC. By BARNARD SMITH. With Answers. Crown 8vo. limp cloth, 2*s.* 6*d.* Or sold separately, as follows :— Part I. 1*s.* Part II. 1*s.* Answers, 6*d.*

SMITH.—SCHOOL CLASS BOOK of ARITHMETIC. By BARNARD SMITH. 18mo. cloth, 3*s.* Or sold separately, Parts I. and II. 10*d.* each, Part III. 1*s.*

SNOWBALL. — THE ELEMENTS of PLANE and SPHERICAL TRIGONOMETRY. By J. C. SNOWBALL, M.A. *Tenth Edition,* Crown 8vo. 7*s.* 6*d.*

SPRING SONGS. — By a WEST HIGHLANDER. With a Vignette Illustration by GOURLAY STEELE. Fcap. 8vo. 1*s.* 6*d.*

STEPHEN. — GENERAL VIEW of the CRIMINAL LAW of ENGLAND. By J. FITZJAMES STEPHEN. 8vo. 18*s.*

STORY.—MEMOIR of the Rev. ROBERT STORY. By R. H. STORY. Crown 8vo. 7*s.* 6*d.*

STRICKLAND.—ON COTTAGE CONSTRUCTION and DESIGN. By C. W. STRICKLAND. With Specifications and Plans. 8vo. 7*s.* 6*d.*

SWAINSON. — A HANDBOOK to BUTLER'S ANALOGY. By C. A. SWAINSON, D.D. Crown 8vo. 1*s.* 6*d.*

SWAINSON.—The CREEDS of the CHURCH in their RELATIONS to HOLY SCRIPTURE and the CONSCIENCE of the CHRISTIAN. 8vo. cloth 9*s.*

SWAINSON.—The AUTHORITY of the NEW TESTAMENT, and other Lectures, delivered before the University of Cambridge. 8vo. cloth, 12*s.*

TACITUS.—The HISTORY of TACITUS translated into ENGLISH. By A. J. CHURCH, M.A., and W. J. BRODRIBB, M.A. With a Map and Notes. 8vo. 10*s.* 6*d.*

TAIT AND STEELE.—A TREATISE ON DYNAMICS, with numerous Examples. By P. G. TAIT and W. J. STEELE. *Second Edition.* Crown 8vo. 10*s.* 6*d.*

TAYLOR.—WORDS AND PLACES; or, Etymological Illustrations of History, Ethnology, and Geography. By the Rev. ISAAC TAYLOR. *Second Edition.* Crown 8vo. 12*s.* 6*d.*

TAYLOR.—THE RESTORATION OF BELIEF. New and Revised Edition. By ISAAC TAYLOR, Esq. Crown 8vo. 8*s.* 6*d.*

TAYLOR.—BALLADS AND SONGS OF BRITTANY. By TOM TAYLOR. With Illustrations by TISSOT, MILLAIS, TENNIEL, KEENE, and H. K. BROWNE. Small 4to. cloth gilt, 12*s.*

TAYLOR. — GEOMETRICAL CONICS. By C. TAYLOR, B.A. Crown 8vo. 7*s.* 6*d.*

TEMPLE. — SERMONS
PREACHED in the CHAPEL
of RUGBY SCHOOL. By F.
TEMPLE, D.D. 8vo. 10s. 6d.

THRING.—A CONSTRU-
ING BOOK. Compiled by
EDWARD THRING, M.A.
Fcap. 8vo. 2s. 6d.

THRING.—A LATIN GRA-
DUAL. A First Latin Constru-
ing Book for Beginners. Fcap.
8vo. 2s. 6d.

THRING.— THE ELE-
MENTS of GRAMMAR taught
in ENGLISH. *Third Edition.*
18mo. 2s.

THRING.—THE CHILD'S
GRAMMAR. *A New Edition.*
18mo. 1s.

THRING. — SERMONS
DELIVERED at UPPINGHAM
SCHOOL. Crown 8vo. 5s.

THRING.—SCHOOL
SONGS. With the Music ar-
ranged for four Voices. Edited
by the Rev. EDWD. THRING,
M.A. and H. RICCIUS. Small
folio, 7s. 6d.

THRING. — EDUCATION
and SCHOOL. By the Rev.
EDWARD THRING, M.A.
Crown 8vo. 6s. 6d.

THRUPP.—The SONG of
SONGS. A New Translation,
with a Commentary and an Introduction. By the Rev. J. F.
THRUPP. Crown 8vo. 7s. 6d.

THRUPP. — ANTIENT
JERUSALEM : a New Investi-
gation into the History, Topo-
graphy, and Plan of the City,
Environs, and Temple. With
Map and Plans. 8vo. 15s.

THRUPP. — INTRODUC-
TION to the STUDY and USE
of the PSALMS. 2 vols. 21s.

THRUPP—PSALMS AND
HYMNS for PUBLIC WOR-
SHIP. Selected and Edited by
the Rev. J. F. THRUPP, M.A.
18mo. 2s. common paper, 1s. 4d.

TOCQUEVILLE. — ME-
MOIR, LETTERS, and RE-
MAINS of ALEXIS DE TOC-
QUEVILLE. Translated from
the French by the Translator of
"Napoleon's Correspondence with
King Joseph." With Numerous
additions, 2 vols. crown 8vo. 21s.

TODD.—THE BOOKS OF
THE VAUDOIS. The Walden-
sian Manuscripts preserved in the
Library of Trinity College, Dub-
lin, with an Appendix by JAMES
HENTHORN TODD, D.D.
Crown 8vo. cloth, 6s.

TODHUNTER. — WORKS
by ISAAC TODHUNTER,
M.A. F.R.S.

EUCLID FOR COLLEGES
AND SCHOOLS. *New Edition.*
18mo. 3s. 6d.

ALGEBRA FOR BEGINNERS.
With numerous Examples. 18mo.
2s. 6d.

A TREATISE ON THE DIF-
FERENTIAL CALCULUS.
With numerous Examples. *Fourth
Edition.* Crown 8vo. 10s 6d.

A TREATISE ON THE IN-
TEGRAL CALCULUS. *Second
Edition.* With numerous Exam-
ples. Crown 8vo. 10s. 6d.

A TREATISE ON ANALYTI-
CAL STATICS. *Second Edition.*
Crown 8vo. 10s. 6d.

A TREATISE ON CONIC SEC-
TIONS. *Third Edition.* Crown
8vo. 7*s.* 6*d.*

ALGEBRA FOR THE USE OF
COLLEGES AND SCHOOLS.
Third Edition. Crown 8vo. 7*s.* 6*d.*

PLANE TRIGONOMETRY for
COLLEGES and SCHOOLS.
Second Edition. Crown 8vo. 5*s.*

A TREATISE ON SPHERICAL
TRIGONOMETRY for the USE
of COLLEGES and SCHOOLS.
Second Edition. Crown 8vo. 4*s.* 6*d.*

CRITICAL HISTORY OF THE
PROGRESS of the CALCULUS
of VARIATIONS during the
NINETEENTH CENTURY.
8vo. 12*s.*

EXAMPLES OF ANALYTICAL
GEOMETRY of THREE DI-
MENSIONS. *Second Edition.*
Crown 8vo. 4*s.*

A TREATISE on the THEORY
of EQUATIONS. Crown 8vo.
cloth, 7*s.* 6*d.*

A HISTORY of the MATHE-
MATICAL THEORY of PRO-
BABILITY. 8vo. cloth, 18*s.*

TOM BROWN'S SCHOOL
DAYS. By an OLD BOY. *29th
Thousand.* Fcap. 8vo. 5*s.* Also
People's Edition. Small 8vo. 2*s.*

TOM BROWN at OXFORD.
By the Author of "Tom Brown's
School Days." *New Edition.*
Crown 8vo. 6*s.*

TRACTS FOR PRIESTS
and PEOPLE. By VARIOUS
WRITERS.

THE FIRST SERIES, Crown
8vo. 8*s.*

THE SECOND SERIES, Crown
8vo. 8*s.*

The whole Series of Fifteen
Tracts may be had separately,
price One Shilling each.

TRENCH. — WORKS BY
R. CHENEVIX TRENCH,
D.D. Archbishop of Dublin.

NOTES ON THE PARABLES
OF OUR LORD. *Ninth Edi-
tion.* 8vo. 12*s.*

NOTES ON THE MIRACLES
OF OUR LORD. *Seventh Edition.* 8vo. 12*s.*

SYNONYMS OF THE NEW
TESTAMENT. *New Edition.*
1 vol. 8vo. cloth, 10*s.* 6*d.*

ON THE STUDY OF WORDS.
Eleventh Edition. Fcap. 4*s.*

ENGLISH PAST AND PRE-
SENT. *Fifth Edition.* Fcap.
8vo. 4*s.*

PROVERBS and their LESSONS.
Fifth Edition. Fcap. 8vo. 3*s.*

SELECT GLOSSARY OF EN-
GLISH WORDS used Formerly
in SENSES different from the
PRESENT. *Second Edition.* 4*s.*

ON SOME DEFICIENCIES IN
our ENGLISH DICTION-
ARIES. *Second Edition.* 8vo. 3*s.*

SERMONS PREACHED IN
WESTMINSTER ABBEY. *Se-
cond Edition.* 8vo. 10*s.* 6*d.*

THE FITNESS OF HOLY
SCRIPTURE for UNFOLDING
the SPIRITUAL LIFE of MAN:
Christ the Desire of all Nations;
or, the Unconscious Prophecies
of Heathendom. Hulsean Lectures. Fcap. 8vo. *Fourth Edition.* 5*s.*

ARCHBISHOP TRENCH'S WORKS (*continued*)—

ON THE AUTHORIZED VERSION of the NEW TESTAMENT. *Second Edition.* 7s.

JUSTIN MARTYR and OTHER POEMS. *Fifth Edition.* Fcap. 8vo. 6s.

POEMS FROM EASTERN SOURCES, GENOVEVA, and other Poems. *Second Edition.* 5s. 6d.

ELEGIAC POEMS. *Third Edition.* 2s. 6d.

CALDERON'S LIFE'S A DREAM : the Great Theatre of the World. With an Essay on his Life and Genius. 4s. 6d.

REMAINS OF THE LATE MRS. RICHARD TRENCH. Being Selections from her Journals, Letters, and other Papers. *Second Edition.* With Portrait, 8vo. 15s.

COMMENTARY ON THE EPISTLES TO THE SEVEN CHURCHES IN ASIA. *Second Edition.* 8s. 6d.

SACRED LATIN POETRY. Chiefly Lyrical. Selected and Arranged for Use. *Second Edition.* Corrected and Improved. Fcap. 8vo. 7s.

TRENCH—BRIEF NOTES on the GREEK of the NEW TESTAMENT (for English Readers). By the Rev. FRANCIS TRENCH, M.A. Crown 8vo. cloth, 6s.

TRENCH.—FOUR ASSIZE SERMONS, Preached at York and Leeds. By the Rev. FRANCIS TRENCH, M.A. Crown 8vo. cloth, 2s. 6d.

TREVELYAN.—THE COMPETITION WALLAH. By G. O. TREVELYAN. Cr. 8vo. 9s.

TREVELYAN.—CAWNPORE. By G. O. TREVELYAN. Illustrated with a Plan and Two Engravings. Crown 8vo. cloth, 10s. 6d.

TUDOR.—THE DECALOGUE VIEWED AS THE CHRISTIAN'S LAW, with Special Reference to the Questions and Wants of the Times. By the Rev. RICH. TUDOR, B.A. Crown 8vo. 10s. 6d.

TULLOCH.—The CHRIST OF THE GOSPELS AND THE CHRIST OF MODERN CRITICISM. Lectures on M. RENAN'S "Vie de Jésus." By JOHN TULLOCH, D.D. Principal of the College of St. Mary, in the University of St. Andrew. Extra fcap. 8vo. 4s. 6d.

TURNER.—SONNETS by the Rev. CHARLES TENNYSON TURNER. Dedicated to his brother, the Poet Laureate. Fcap. 8vo. 4s. 6d.

TYRWHITT.—THE SCHOOLING OF LIFE. By R. St. JOHN TYRWHITT, M.A. Vicar of St. Mary Magdalen, Oxford. Fcap. 8vo. 3s. 6d.

VACATION TOURISTS ; and Notes of Travel in 1861. Edited by F. GALTON, F.R.S. With Ten Maps illustrating the Routes. 8vo. 14s.

VACATION TOURISTS ; and Notes of Travel in 1862 and 3. Edited by FRANCIS GALTON, F.R.S. 8vo. 16s.

VAUGHAN. — SERMONS PREACHED in ST. JOHN'S CHURCH, LEICESTER, during the Years 1855 and 1856. By DAVID J. VAUGHAN, M.A. Vicar of St. Martin's, Leicester. Crown 8vo. 5s. 6d.

VAUGHAN. — SERMONS ON THE RESURRECTION. With a Preface. By D. J. VAUGHAN, M.A. Fcap. 8vo. 3s.

VAUGHAN.—THREE SERMONS ON THE ATONEMENT. By D. J. VAUGHAN, M.A. 1s. 6d.

VAUGHAN. — SERMONS ON SACRIFICE AND PROPITIATION. By D. J. VAUGHAN, M.A. 2s. 6d.

VAUGHAN.—CHRISTIAN EVIDENCES and the BIBLE. By DAVID J. VAUGHAN, M.A. Fcap. 8vo. cloth, price 3s. 6d.

VAUGHAN.—WORKS BY CHARLES J. VAUGHAN, D.D. Vicar of Doncaster :—

NOTES FOR LECTURES ON CONFIRMATION. With suitable Prayers. *Sixth Edition.* 1s. 6d.

LECTURES on the EPISTLE to the PHILIPPIANS. *Second Edition.* 7s. 6d.

LECTURES on the REVELATION of ST. JOHN. 2 vols. crown 8vo. 15s. *Second Edition.* 15s.

EPIPHANY, LENT, AND EASTER. A Selection of Expository Sermons. *Second Edition.* Crown 8vo. 10s. 6d.

THE BOOK AND THE LIFE: and other Sermons Preached before the University of Cambridge. *Second Edition.* Fcap. 8vo. 4s. 6d.

MEMORIALS OF HARROW SUNDAYS. A Selection of Sermons preached in Harrow School Chapel. With a View of the Chapel. *Fourth Edition.* Cr. 8vo. 10s. 6d.

ST. PAUL'S EPISTLE TO THE ROMANS. The Greek Text with English Notes. *Second Edition.* Crown 8vo. red leaves, 5s.

REVISION OF THE LITURGY. Four Discourses. With an Introduction. I. ABSOLUTISM. II. REGENERATION. III. ATHANASIAN CREED. IV. BURIAL SERVICE. V. HOLY ORDERS. *Second Edit.* Cr. 8vo. red leaves, 4s. 6d.

LESSONS OF LIFE AND GODLINESS. A Selection of Sermons Preached in the Parish Church of Doncaster. *Third Edition.* Fcap. 8vo. 4s. 6d.

WORDS from the GOSPELS. A Second Selection of Sermons Preached in the Parish Church of Doncaster. *Second Edition.* Fcap. 8vo. 4s. 6d.

THE EPISTLES of ST. PAUL. For English Readers. Part I. containing the First Epistle to the Thessalonians. 8vo. 1s. 6d. Each Epistle will be published separately.

THE CHURCH OF THE FIRST DAYS :—
    Series I. The Church of Jerusalem.
      ,, II. The Church of the Gentiles.
      ,, III. The Church of the World.
    Fcap. 8vo. cloth, 4s. 6d. each.

LIFE'S WORK AND GOD'S DISCIPLINE. Three Sermons. Fcap. 8vo. cloth, 2s. 6d.

VAUGHAN.—MEMOIR of ROBERT A. VAUGHAN, Author of " Hours with the Mystics." By ROB. VAUGHAN, D.D. *Second Edition.* Revised and enlarged. Extra fcap. 8vo. 5s.

VILLAGE SERMONS BY A NORTHAMPTONSHIRE RECTOR. With a Preface on the Inspiration of Holy Scripture. Crown 8vo. 6s.

VIRGIL. — THE ÆNEID Translated into English Blank VERSE. By JOHN MILLER. Crown 8vo. 10s. 6d.

VOLUNTEER'S SCRAP BOOK. By the Author of " The Cambridge Scrap Book." Crown 4to. 7s. 6d.

WAGNER.—MEMOIR OF THE REV. GEORGE WAGNER, late of St. Stephen's, Brighton. By J. N. SIMPKINSON, M.A. *Third and Cheaper Edition.* 5s.

WATSON AND ROUTH.— CAMBRIDGE SENATE-HOUSE PROBLEMS AND RIDERS. For the Year 1860. With Solutions by H. W. WATSON, M.A. and E. J. ROUTH, M.A. Cr. 8vo. 7s. 6d.

WARREN.—AN ESSAY on GREEK FEDERAL COINAGE. By the Hon. J. LEICESTER WARREN, M.A. 8vo. 2s. 6d.

WESTCOTT. — HISTORY of the CANON of the NEW TESTAMENT during the First Four Centuries. By BROOKE FOSS WESTCOTT, M.A. Cr. 8vo. 12s. 6d.

WESTCOTT. — CHARACTERISTICS of the GOSPEL MIRACLES. Sermons Preached before the University of Cambridge. *With Notes.* By B. F. WESTCOTT, M.A. Crown 8vo. 4s. 6d.

WESTCOTT. — INTRODUCTION TO THE STUDY OF THE FOUR GOSPELS. By B. F. WESTCOTT, M.A. Crown 8vo. 10s. 6d.

WESTCOTT.—The BIBLE in the CHURCH. A Popular Account of the Collection and Reception of the Holy Scriptures in the Christian Churches. By B. F. WESTCOTT, M.A. 18mo. 4s. 6d.

WESTMINSTER PLAYS.— Sive Prologi et Epilogi ad Fabulas in Sti Petri Colleg: actas qui Exstabant collecti et justa quoad licuit annorum serie ordinati, quibus accedit Declamationum qui vocantur et Epigrammatum delectus cur. F. MURE, A.M., H. BULL, A.M., CAROLO B. SCOTT, B.D. 8vo. 12s. 6d.

WILSON.—COUNSELS OF AN INVALID : Letters on Religious Subjects. By GEORGE WILSON, M. D. With Vignette Portrait. Fcap. 8vo. 4s. 6d.

WILSON.—RELIGIO CHEMICI. By GEORGE WILSON, M. D. With a Vignette beautifully engraved after a Design by NOEL PATON. Crown 8vo. 8s. 6d.

WILSON — MEMOIR OF GEORGE WILSON, M. D. F. R. S. E. Regius Professor of Technology in the University of Edinburgh. By his Sister. Third Thousand. 8vo. with Portrait, 10s. 6d.

WILSON. — THE FIVE GATEWAYS OF KNOWLEDGE. By GEORGE WILSON, M.D. *New Edit.* Fcap. 8vo. 2s. 6d. or in Paper Covers, 1s.

WILSON.—The PROGRESS of the TELEGRAPH. Fcap. 8vo. 1s.

WILSON.—PREHISTORIC ANNALS of SCOTLAND. By DANIEL WILSON, LL.D. Author of "Prehistoric Man," &c. 2 vols. demy 8vo. *New Edition.* With numerous Illustrations. 36s.

WILSON.—PREHISTORIC MAN. By DANIEL WILSON, LL.D. *New Edition.* Revised and partly re-written, with numerous Illustrations. 1 vol. 8vo.

WILSON. — A TREATISE ON DYNAMICS. By W. P. WILSON, M.A. 8vo. 9s. 6d.

WILTON.—THE NEGEB; or, "South Country" of Scripture. By the Rev. E. WILTON, M.A. Crown 8vo. 7s. 6d.

WOLFE.—ONE HUNDRED AND FIFTY ORIGINAL PSALM AND HYMN TUNES. For Four Voices. By ARTHUR WOLFE, M.A. 10s. 6d.

WOLFE. — HYMNS FOR PUBLIC WORSHIP. Selected and arranged by ARTHUR WOLFE, M.A. 18mo. 2s. Common Paper Edition, 1s. or twenty-five for 1l.

WOLFE. — HYMNS FOR PRIVATE USE.—Selected and arranged by ARTHUR WOLFE, M.A. 18mo. 2s.

WOODFORD.—CHRISTIAN SANCTITY. By JAMES RUSSELL WOODFORD, M.A. Fcap. 8vo. cloth. 3s.

WOODWARD. — ESSAYS, THOUGHTS and REFLECTIONS, and LETTERS. By the Rev. HENRY WOODWARD. Edited by his Son. *Fifth Edition.* 8vo. cloth. 10s. 6d.

WOODWARD.—THE SHUNAMITE. By the Rev. HENRY WOODWARD, M.A. Edited by his Son, THOMAS WOODWARD, M.A. Dean of Down. *Second Edition.* Crown 8vo. cloth. 10s. 6d.

WOOLLEY. — LECTURES DELIVERED IN AUSTRALIA. By JOHN WOOLLEY, D.C.L. Crown 8vo. 8s. 6d.

WOOLNER. — MY BEAUTIFUL LADY. By THOMAS WOOLNER. *Second Edition.* Fcap. 8vo. 5s.

WORSHIP (THE) OF GOD AND FELLOWSHIP AMONG MEN—Sermons on Public Worship. By MAURICE and Others. Fcap. 8vo. cloth. 3s. 6d.

WRIGHT.—HELLENICA; or, a History of Greece in Greek, as related by Diodorus and Thucydides, being a First Greek Reading Book, with Explanatory Notes, Critical and Historical. By J. WRIGHT, M.A. *Second Edition,* WITH A VOCABULARY. 12mo. 3s. 6d.

WRIGHT.—A HELP TO LATIN GRAMMAR; or, the Form and Use of Words in Latin. With Progressive Exercises. Cr. 8vo. 4s. 6d.

WRIGHT. — THE SEVEN KINGS OF ROME: An Easy Narrative, abridged from the First Book of Livy by the omission of difficult passages, being a First Latin Reading Book, with Grammatical Notes. Fcap. 8vo. 3s.

WRIGHT. — A VOCABULARY AND EXERCISES ON THE "SEVEN KINGS OF ROME." Fcap. 8vo. 2s. 6d.

** The Vocabulary and Exercises may also be had bound up with "The Seven Kings of Rome." 5s.

WRIGHT.—DAVID, KING OF ISRAEL: Readings for the Young. By J. WRIGHT, M.A. With Six Illustrations. Royal 16mo. cloth, gilt. 3s. 6d.

WORKS BY THE AUTHOR OF
"THE HEIR OF REDCLYFFE."

A BOOK OF GOLDEN DEEDS. 18mo. 4s. 6d.

THE TRIAL; More Links of the Daisy Chain. *Second Edition.* Crown 8vo. 6s.

HISTORY OF CHRISTIAN NAMES. Two Vols. Crown 8vo. 1l. 1s.

THE HEIR OF REDCLYFFE. *Fourteenth Edition.* Crown 8vo. 6s.

DYNEVOR TERRACE. *Third Edition.* Crown 8vo. 6s.

THE DAISY CHAIN. *Seventh Edition.* Crown 8vo. 6s.

HEART'S EASE. *Eighth Edition.* Crown 8vo. 6s.

HOPES AND FEARS. *Second Edition.* Crown 8vo. 6s.

THE YOUNG STEPMOTHER. Crown 8vo. 6s.

THE LANCES OF LYNWOOD. 18mo. cloth, 3s. 6d.

THE LITTLE DUKE. *New Edition.* 18mo. cloth, 3s. 6d.

CLEVER WOMAN OF THE FAMILY. 2 vols. 12s.

LONDON: R. CLAY, SON, AND TAYLOR, PRINTERS.